School Supports for Students in Military Families

The Guilford Practical Intervention in the Schools Series

Kenneth W. Merrell, *Founding Editor*
Sandra M. Chafouleas, *Series Editor*

www.guilford.com/practical

This series presents the most reader-friendly resources available in key areas of evidence-based practice in school settings. Practitioners will find trustworthy guides on effective behavioral, mental health, and academic interventions, and assessment and measurement approaches. Covering all aspects of planning, implementing, and evaluating high-quality services for students, books in the series are carefully crafted for everyday utility. Features include ready-to-use reproducibles, appealing visual elements, and an oversized format. Recent titles have Web pages where purchasers can download and print the reproducible materials.

Recent Volumes

High-Impact Assessment Reports for Children and Adolescents:
A Consumer-Responsive Approach
Robert Lichtenstein and Bruce Ecker

Conducting School-Based Functional Behavioral Assessments, Third Edition:
A Practitioner's Guide
*Mark W. Steege, Jamie L. Pratt, Garry Wickerd, Richard Guare,
and T. Steuart Watson*

Evaluating Educational Interventions, Second Edition:
Single-Case Design for Measuring Response to Intervention
T. Chris Riley-Tillman, Matthew K. Burns, and Stephen P. Kilgus

The Data-Driven School: Collaborating to Improve Student Outcomes
*Daniel M. Hyson, Joseph F. Kovaleski, Benjamin Silberglitt,
and Jason A. Pedersen*

Implementing Classwide PBIS: A Guide to Supporting Teachers
Diane Myers, Brandi Simonsen, and Jennifer Freeman

Social and Emotional Learning in the Classroom, Second Edition:
Promoting Mental Health and Academic Success
Barbara A. Gueldner, Laura L. Feuerborn, and Kenneth W. Merrell

Responding to Problem Behavior in Schools, Third Edition:
The Check-In, Check-Out Intervention
*Leanne S. Hawken, Deanne A. Crone, Kaitlin Bundock,
and Robert H. Horner*

School-Based Behavioral Assessment, Second Edition:
Informing Prevention and Intervention
*Sandra M. Chafouleas, Austin H. Johnson, T. Chris Riley-Tillman,
and Emily A. Iovino*

Child and Adolescent Suicidal Behavior, Second Edition:
School-Based Prevention, Assessment, and Intervention
David N. Miller

School Supports for Students in Military Families
Pamela Fenning

School Supports for Students in Military Families

PAMELA FENNING

THE GUILFORD PRESS
New York   London

Copyright © 2021 The Guilford Press
A Division of Guilford Publications, Inc.
370 Seventh Avenue, Suite 1200, New York, NY 10001
www.guilford.com

All rights reserved

Except as indicated, no part of this book may be reproduced, translated, stored in a retrieval system, or transmitted, in any form or by any means, electronic, mechanical, photocopying, microfilming, recording, or otherwise, without written permission from the publisher.

Printed in the United States of America

This book is printed on acid-free paper.

Last digit is print number: 9 8 7 6 5 4 3 2 1

LIMITED DUPLICATION LICENSE

These materials are intended for use only by qualified professionals.

The publisher grants to individual purchasers of this book nonassignable permission to reproduce all materials for which permission is specifically granted in a footnote. This license is limited to you, the individual purchaser, for personal use or use with students. This license does not grant the right to reproduce these materials for resale, redistribution, electronic display, or any other purposes (including but not limited to books, pamphlets, articles, video- or audiotapes, blogs, file-sharing sites, Internet or intranet sites, and handouts or slides for lectures, workshops, or webinars, whether or not a fee is charged). Permission to reproduce these materials for these and any other purposes must be obtained in writing from the Permissions Department of Guilford Publications.

The author has checked with sources believed to be reliable in her efforts to provide information that is complete and generally in accord with the standards of practice that are accepted at the time of publication. However, in view of the possibility of human error or changes in behavioral, mental health, or medical sciences, neither the author, nor the editors and publisher, nor any other party who has been involved in the preparation or publication of this work warrants that the information contained herein is in every respect accurate or complete, and they are not responsible for any errors or omissions or the results obtained from the use of such information. Readers are encouraged to confirm the information contained in this book with other sources.

Library of Congress Cataloging-in-Publication Data

Names: Fenning, Pamela, author.
Title: School supports for students in military families / Pamela Fenning.
Description: New York ; London : The Guilford Press, [2021] | Series: The Guilford Practical
   Intervention in the Schools Series | Includes bibliographical references and index. |
Identifiers: LCCN 2021027361 | ISBN 9781462546930 (Paperback : acid-free paper) |
   ISBN 9781462546947 (Hardcover : acid-free paper)
Subjects: LCSH: Children of military personnel—Education—United States. |
   School psychology—United States—Case studies. | Military dependents—United States—
   Psychology. | Families of military personnel—United States—Social conditions. | Child
   development. | BISAC: PSYCHOLOGY / Psychotherapy / Child & Adolescent | EDUCATION /
   Educational Psychology
Classification: LCC LC5081 .F46 2021 | DDC 370.15—dc23
LC record available at *https://lccn.loc.gov/202102736*

*This book is dedicated to the memory of my dad, David N. Fenning,
a military veteran who was a gentle giant with a heart of gold.
It is also dedicated to the military families in my own community,
whom I have the honor and privilege of calling friends and neighbors.*

About the Author

Pamela Fenning, PhD, ABPP, is Professor of School Psychology at Loyola University Chicago. She is a licensed clinical and school psychologist in Illinois and holds board certification in School Psychology. Dr. Fenning's research and clinical work focus on multi-tiered academic and behavioral interventions at the high school level, systems-level interventions, equity and ethnic disproportionality in school-discipline policy, evaluation of alternatives-to-suspension programs, high-risk behaviors of adolescents, competency training in school-psychology professional preparation programs, and support of military families.

Contents

1. **Strengths and Needs of Military Youth and Their Families in Schools: The Role of School Psychologists**   1
   Prevalence of School-Age Military Youth   1
   Military Deployments of Service Members with Families   2
   Guidance for Schools in Supporting Military Children and Families   2
   The Role of School Psychologists in Supporting Military Youth and Families   2
   Features of a Strengths-Based/Resiliency Approach   3
       Strengths-Based Approach   3
       Resiliency Approach   4
   Multi-Tiered Systems of Support   5
       MTSS Applications to Military Youth and Families   6
       Specific Functions of School Psychologists in MTSS Data-Based Decision Making   7
   Overview of the Chapters to Follow   10

2. **Educational Settings Attended by Military Youth: Contextual Considerations and Case Studies**   11
   Overview of School Environments That Educate Military Youth   11
       Public Schools/Civilian Settings   11
       DoD Schools   12
       Non-DoD Schools   12
   Public Schools/Civilian Settings   12
       Awareness of Public School Military Students and Use of Military Student Identifiers   13
       Social Support of Military Students in Public School Environments   14
       Local Context and Community Cultural Considerations   16
       Fictional Family Snapshot in a Public School Environment   16
   DoD Schools   17
       Accreditation   17
       Graduation Requirements   18

Academic Achievement in DoD Schools 19
Characteristics of DoD Schools 20
Fictional Family Snapshot in a DoD School 21
Non-DoD Schools 22
Fictional Family Snapshot in a Non-DoD-Administered School 24
Conclusion 25

3. Universal Screening Data and Multi-Tiered Systems of Support for Military Children   27

General Principles of MTSS 27
Universal Screening as a Major MTSS Practice 28
   Academic Screening 28
   Behavioral/Social–Emotional Screening 28
Application of Decision Rules 29
Universal/Tier 1 Screening and Support with Military Youth 30
   Defining Military-Connected School-Age Youth 31
   Data Collection Specific to Military Youth 32
Procedural Considerations for Universal Screening and Support with Military Youth 33
Practice Considerations for Universal/Tier 1 Screening and Support with Military Youth 34
Problem-Solving Considerations for Universal/Tier 1 Screening and Support for Military Youth 34
   Consideration 1 35
   Consideration 2 36
   Consideration 3 36
Special Considerations for Secondary/Tier 2 Systems of Support with Military Youth 38
Special Considerations for Tertiary/Tier 3 Systems of Support with Military Youth 39
Case Example of a Universal Screening/MTSS Approach in a Civilian Middle School 40
Form 3.1. Family Military Service and Brief Educational History 43

4. Promoting Healthy Social Development   46

Impact of Military Transitions on Social Development and Relationships 46
Social Supports with Military Youth and Families: One Size Does Not Fit All 47
Applications of Social Developmental Theory with Military Youth 48
   Social Development in Infancy and Early Childhood 48
   Social Development during the Elementary School Years 51
   Social Development during Adolescence 55
Overall Social Development Supports for Military Youth across the Developmental Spectrum and Conclusions 60

5. Delivery of Mental Health Supports   61

Tier 1/Universal Mental Health Applications 61
   Social Relationships and Connections 61
   School Climate 64
   Universal and Classroom-Based Social–Emotional Learning Approaches 65
Addressing the Specialized Needs of Military Youth: Tier 2 and Tier 3 Applications 67
   Cognitive-Behavioral Interventions 68
Tier 3 Intensive Supports: Wraparound Planning 71
Military Deployments: Special Considerations for School Psychologists 71
   Deployment Characteristics and Family/Youth Mental Health 74
   Assessments of Emotional and Behavioral Concerns in Deployment Situations 75
   Risk of Child Maltreatment 75
   Family Stressors and Dynamics across the Deployment Cycle 76
   Support for Military Families and Youth Experiencing Deployment 77

Case Example of Individualized Family Supports in Meadowood Elementary and Allen Middle School   78
Conclusion   81

6. Support during School Transitions   82
with Gina Coffee
Military Families' Experiences Transitioning between Schools   84
The Military Interstate Children's Compact   84
Special Considerations in Transitions of Military Youth with Disabilities   85
  The Exceptional Family Member Program   87
Extracurricular Activities   90
The Role of the School Psychologist in Supporting Students during Transitions   91
Critical Functions and Roles of School Psychologists in Supporting Transitions   92
Consultation and Collaboration Lens   94
Conclusion   98

7. Legal Aspects of School Supports for Military Youth   99
Every Student Succeeds Act   100
  Accountability and Data Requirements   100
  Disaggregated-Subgroup Military Data   100
  Specialized Instructional Support Personnel Defined   101
  Impact Aid   102
  Special Education Legislation and Provisions   103
  DoD-Specific Special Education Regulations   103
National Defense Authorization Act   104
Military Interstate Children's Compact   105
  Case Examples Illustrating the Application of the Military Interstate Children's Compact
Conclusion   110
Appendix 7.1. Information on Accessing Special Education and Legal Resources Described in This Chapter   111

8. Conclusions and Future Directions   112
Overall Summary and Concluding Comments   119

References   121

Index   137

Purchasers of this book can download and print
the Family Military Service and Brief Educational History form
at *www.guilford.com/fenning-forms* for personal use or use
with students (see copyright page for details).

CHAPTER 1

Strengths and Needs of Military Youth and Their Families in Schools
The Role of School Psychologists

PREVALENCE OF SCHOOL-AGE MILITARY YOUTH

There are over 2 million active-duty and selected reserve military members who make enormous personal sacrifices to protect our safety, as do the over 2.7 million military family members who include spouses, children, and adult dependents (U.S. Department of Defense [DoD], 2016). Over 40% of military personnel have children (U.S. DoD, 2016). A demographics profile of school-age military children and their families includes the following detailed statistics:

- Military youth are found across all grade levels, with most being under age 5 (42.2%). Nearly 32% of military children are between the ages of 6 and 11, and nearly 22% are adolescents between the ages of 12 and 18 (DoD, 2016).
- According to the School Superintendents Association (2019), there are 1.4 million estimated active-duty military members and roughly 810,000 individuals in the National Guard and Reserves. Families in the National Guard and Reserves do not typically live in proximity to military bases, and, as a result, do not have the same access to military supports as do active military personnel (School Superintendents Association, 2019).
- Among selected reserve members, over 32.5% are married with children, and 9.1% are single parents. Specific to selected reserve members, school-age children constitute the highest percentage of dependent children (31.2%), followed by children ages 5 and younger (31.2%) and adolescents (27%).
- Military youth are most likely to attend Civilian public schools rather than DoD-

operated schools (Astor, De Pedro, Gilreath, Esqueda, & Benbenishty, 2013; De Pedro, et al. 2011). In Civilian public schools, there may not be an awareness among school personnel that their students include military youth, which elevates the risk that these youth are not being properly educated and supported.

MILITARY DEPLOYMENTS OF SERVICE MEMBERS WITH FAMILIES

Modern-day military families who have served in Iraq and Afghanistan have experienced the most frequent and longest deployments since World War II (Chandra et al., 2011, as cited in Esposito-Smythers et al., 2011). The "new normal" of frequent and lengthy deployments has implications that have yet to be understood for military youth and their families.

- Nearly half of military parents serving in these wars have had at least two deployments (Lester et al., 2013).
- The long-term outcome of these extensive deployments for today's military youth and their families is largely unknown (Flake, Davis, Johnson, & Middleton, 2009), particularly with respect to school-related success (Astor et al., 2013; De Pedro et al., 2011).

GUIDANCE FOR SCHOOLS IN SUPPORTING MILITARY CHILDREN AND FAMILIES

Arguably, the most prolific military researchers whose work has direct implications for school-based professionals have been affiliated with the consortium *Building Capacity and Welcoming Practices in Military-Connected Schools* at the University of Southern California (USC) School of Social Work (Astor et al., 2013; De Pedro et al., 2011). The collective work of these researchers is contained in four practical guides about the education of military youth (Astor, Jacobson, Benbenishty, Pineda, & Atuel, 2012a, 2012b, 2012c). There are guides written specifically for teachers (Astor et al., 2012a), school administrators (Astor et al., 2012b), and pupil services personnel (e.g., psychologists, social workers, and counselors; Astor et al., 2012c). There is also a specific guide for military families, which offers recommendations for supporting them as advocates for their children's education (Astor, Jacobson, Benbenishty, Pineda, & Atuel, 2012d).

THE ROLE OF SCHOOL PSYCHOLOGISTS IN SUPPORTING MILITARY YOUTH AND FAMILIES

School psychologists are in a unique position to build upon the important work being done by other mental and behavioral mental health professionals (Astor et al., 2013; De Pedro et al., 2011) since they work in all types of schools, particularly in Civilian schools where most military children are educated (Astor et al., 2013; De Pedro et al., 2011). Given their training in areas such as family–school collaboration, mental health, diverse preventive and responsive services, problem solving, interventions, systems of support, data-based decision making, and program evaluation (Skalski et al., 2015), school psychologists are ideally qualified to take a *strengths-based/resiliency approach within a multi-tiered framework* in providing comprehensive supports to military youth and their families.

FEATURES OF A STRENGTHS-BASED/RESILIENCY APPROACH

Strengths-Based Approach

I argue for a strengths-based approach in supporting military families because although this approach is understudied in the literature, military families and their school-age children possess many strengths and assets that need to be understood by school psychologists and other school-based professionals (Lerner, Almerigi, Theokas, & Lerner, 2005; Lerner, Zaff, & Lerner, 2009). Military family strengths and assets include the ability to maintain emotional family closeness despite separation, their sense of honor and duty, and their values (Lerner et al., 2009). The strengths can be enhanced through community, school, and family resources that align with these assets (Lerner et al., 2009). School psychologists can provide a valuable service by helping military families, who may have just moved into a community, to access such resources. Military youth show other strengths that include a greater respect for authority and an openness to differences that may materialize as a willingness to make friends at school with those viewed as different (Easterbrooks, Ginsburg, & Lerner, 2013; Hall, 2008, as cited in Park, 2011). Easterbrooks and colleagues (2013), in their analysis of the resiliency of military youth during the Iraq and Afghanistan wars, found that military youth are less likely to engage in risky behavior. Furthermore, while extended deployments can certainly result in significant stress and related mental health concerns (Flake et al., 2009), Easterbrooks et al. (2013) contend that deployment situations have the potential to bring families closer and promote independence and increased responsibility. Other strengths are the likelihood that military youth have not only a strong connection to their families, but also to their communities as well, particularly when facing similar challenges and experiences (Easterbrooks et al., 2013).

Speaking specifically about the role of the school psychologist in supporting the needs of military youth, Sherman and Glenn (2011) cite their additional strengths, such as having a sense of duty and commitment to teamwork, which are critical for success within a military environment. Taking a strengths-based/resiliency approach means that school psychologists honor and foster the many gifts and strengths that military youth and their families bring to schools through their personal lived experiences, including those connected with military service (Masten, 2001; Park, 2011). From a school psychology perspective, a strengths-based/resiliency approach is realized by carefully listening to the concerns voiced by military youth and and their families when determining how to support their educational, social, and mental health needs. Rather than determining what should be "done with" military youth as they transition in and out of school settings, a strengths-based/resiliency approach dispels the myth that they are needy or a burden to schools. The empirical literature documents that military youth function very well academically, even better than their Civilian peers (Park, 2011, as cited in Easterbrooks et al., 2013). Military youth and their families may simply need the right support at the right time to be successful in navigating educational environments, while also navigating other aspects of military life, such as frequent moves and school transitions (Fenning, Harris, & Viellieu, 2013). Furthermore, the support of school psychologists and other school professionals may also be warranted when the family is facing the impending deployment of a parent, especially deployments that are of longer durations (Flake et al., 2009; Richardson et al., 2011).

Resiliency Approach

School psychologists can additionally draw upon the psychological literature on resiliency when thinking about how to best support military youth and their families. Masten (2001) argues that resiliency is not extraordinary behavior on the part of individuals, but rather "a common phenomenon that results in most cases from the operation of the human adaptational system" (p. 227). Masten (2001) further stresses that resiliency is based on "ordinary" (p. 227) developmental processes. Easterbrooks et al. (2013), define *resiliency* as a bidirectional process that involves the interaction of an individual with his or her environment and apply the concept to military youth. They state, "The relations between an individual and his or her context produce resilience" (p. 100). Easterbrooks et al. (2013) further specify that resiliency operates in much the same manner for military-involved youth as their Civilian peers in a similar two-way process with fluid individual and environmental interactions. The expression of resiliency in one context or situation does not necessarily result in the expression of the same coping strategies under different environmental conditions (Easterbrooks et al., 2013). Easterbrooks and colleagues further argue that it is important for practitioners to be mindful that military youth face stressors unrelated to military life that are similar to the ones experienced by their non-military involved peers, with the exception of the deployment cycle. School psychologists should consider military youth as individuals and not assume that they are only defined by their connection with the military. They benefit from developmental guidance similar to their Civilian peers, yet owing to the demands of military life, may also need the right supports at key moments, such as when transitioning into or out of a school. Military youth and their families may also need support during other critical times, such as during the deployment cycle. School psychologists, who are positioned in schools with access to military youth, can meet this need and provide general developmental guidance in the life of the military family.

Relatedly, Masten (2013b) argues for the potential application of developmental systems theory (DST) in supporting military families. DST models are based on the notion that child and adolescent development is tied to the multiple contexts in which children and adolescents function, including classrooms, the family unit, larger communities, and societal structures (Masten, 2013b). Applied to military families, the developmental timing of different events and stressors can differentially impact individual child functioning and the larger family system (Masten, 2013b). School psychologists should be aware not only of the stressors faced by military children and their families, but also carefully consider the developmental stage of the military youth at the time and provide a developmentally appropriate response. As an example, during a parental military deployment, the consultation that school psychologists have with colleagues about how to support the military youth would differ, depending on whether a deployment occurs in early childhood/preschool, elementary school, or middle or high school, given the developmental differences in cognition, social understanding, and affect (Masten, 2013b). At the same time, school psychologists should understand that individual military youth and families have different stressors outside of military life, varied support systems, diverse cultural beliefs, and so forth. School psychologists should have an understanding of the fluid and reciprocal nature of developmental stages, as well as individual differences, and not apply a "one-size-fits-all" response to their interactions with military youth and their families. DST is aligned with a strengths-based/resiliency approach because military youth are seen as young people first with developmental needs that should be normalized as part of growing up and not automatically pathologized because they are connected with the military. School psychologists can help to deliver a strengths-based/resiliency approach that meets military youth at their level of development and treats them as individuals (Cozza, Lerner, & Haskins, 2014; De Pedro et al., 2011; Masten, 2013b). They can most efficiently support military families and youth by facilitating prevention-oriented programs and interventions, delivered in schools and facilitated by school–community collaborations along a continuum of support (Adelman, 1996). The continuum of support most aligned with this approach is multi-tiered systems of support (MTSS) (Brown-Chidsey & Andren, 2013). We recommend MTSS as the preferred framework for military youth because it is a data-driven model of efficiency that is widely implemented in schools nationwide. School psychologists are among the leaders of MTSS development and implementation across the country and are uniquely positioned to adopt and adapt MTSS for use with military youth and their families (Brown-Chidsey & Andren, 2013; State of Florida, 2012).

MULTI-TIERED SYSTEMS OF SUPPORT

Chapter 3 focuses on the MTSS process specific to military youth and the role of school psychologists in the process. Stated briefly, MTSS are models of educational service delivery in which problem-solving school-based teams, often facilitated by school psychologists and other specialists trained in data-based decision making, determine, deliver, and evaluate academic, behavioral, and social–emotional supports for all students on a schoolwide system level (universal; Tier 1), and when data findings warrant it, to groups of students as supplements to universal/Tier 1 supports (secondary; Tier 2) and/or in a more robust individualized manner with students who have the most intensive needs (tertiary; Tier 3). Formative assessment data are collected on a routine and ongoing basis to determine how instruction and interventions are working and to fluidly move students across tiers of support as needed, based on data analysis (State of Florida's MTSS, 2012). Curriculum-based measures (CBMs), such as those used as reading screeners, are commonly used in systemwide academic screening processes that typically occur routinely three times per year (Shinn, 2010). Decisions are made on the basis of these data to determine the percentage of students who do not meet established Tier 1 benchmarks and would benefit from supplemental supports (Tier 2, secondary) and/or the most intensive Tier 3 (tertiary) supports (Shinn, 2010). On the behavioral front, schoolwide positive behavior support (SWPBS) has a parallel approach that prioritizes using data to deliver and evaluate systemwide behavior supports for the entire school population. SWPBS practice includes systemwide development, the direct teaching and acknowledgment of behavioral supports, and a systematic manner of collecting and reviewing behavioral data to monitor student responsiveness (Horner, Sugai, & Anderson, 2010; Sandomierski, Kincaid, & Algozzine, 2007). MTSS and relatedly, SWPBS, focus on the performance of the entire school population so that universal system-level core curricula and interventions, whether in the academic, behavioral, or social domain, are as robust as necessary to meet the needs of the largest percentage possible within the school setting, often defined as at least 80% of the school population (Brown, Steege, & Bickford, 2014).

MTSS Applications to Military Youth and Families

MTSS models focus on how particular subgroups within a school population are responding to the universal core curriculum and other interventions that have been determined by a school team as sufficient to meet the school-related needs of youth who require more intensive supports (State of Florida, 2012). Because MTSS approaches are increasingly being used to evaluate outcomes with subpopulations of students, they are highly applicable for use with military youth. Gilreath, Estrada, Peneda, Benbenishty, and Astor (2014) recommend a public health model aligned with MTSS, and from which MTSS is derived, that uses disaggregated data collected specifically on military youth to drive prevention-oriented interventions and programming. School psychologists can apply their knowledge of and experience with MTSS by increasing attention on data collection with subgroups of military youth in their schools and by using the findings to deliver contextually relevant interventions and supports (Brown-Chidsey & Andren, 2013; Burns & Gibbons, 2012).

Highly promising and relevant research and practical applications that directly align with the data-based decision-making components of MTSS are already being conducted. Examples in the military literature show the value of collecting and systematically analyzing school-based data disaggregated by military youth (Chandra & London, 2013, as cited in Cozza, et al., 2014; Cozza et al., 2014; Gilreath et al., 2014). School psychologists, as the data-based decision making experts in the schools, can be instrumental in broadening this work and evaluating it on a systemwide national level. In California, Gilreath and colleagues (2014) reported preliminary findings from a statewide survey, The California

Healthy Kids Survey (CalSCHLS), which contains modules developed specifically to survey military youth. The version for military youth covers youth perspective about school climate, military-related stressors, school safety, and personal wellness. A parent version contains items about their families' military history, how schools were chosen for their children, and their satisfaction with their schools' sensitivity to their military service. The content in the staff version focuses on how sensitive and understanding school personnel are about the lives of military youth. Schools in participating districts can select their preferred modules; these districts have collaborated with USC building-capacity personnel to review the data and set priorities for intervention and programming for military youth. One promising outcome of the data sharing and analysis was a focus on mental health interventions for military-connected youth (Gilreath et al., 2014). The modules are copyright protected and cannot be reproduced without permission. However, they can be viewed at the CalSCHLS website (*https://calschls.org/survey-administration/downloads/#ssm_mcs*).

Specific Functions of School Psychologists in MTSS Data-Based Decision Making

Given that school psychologists can follow military youth during the time they attend school in a particular district, and can help facilitate, with parental or guardian permission, the release of informative academic and other school-based data if students transition to other schools, a database can be generated that can inform long-term outcome data and developmental milestones consistent with the need to have a better understanding of military youth development over time (Cozza et al., 2014). Here is where school psychologists can make data-driven practices with military youth a norm in schools across the country. One specific area in which school psychologists can apply their data-based decision-making skills as part of MTSS practices is with young children in military families, who comprise a large percentage of the military population (DoD, 2016). We offer a research-based illustration pertaining to young children here.

Early Childhood Data Collection

Cozza and colleagues (2014) point out that, although the knowledge base about standard developmental changes across all ages and stages is limited, normative data on young preschool children are particularly scant. School-based professionals, such as school psychologists, school social workers, speech and language clinicians, and others involved with screening for early intervention as part of federally mandated Child Find procedures (Wright & Wright, 2008), could make an invaluable contribution to the profession in supporting young military children. An initial basic step, which has not been widely adopted, would be for the school or district conducting the screening to track demographic and academic screening information about the military status of families (Cozza et al., 2014; Garcia, De Pedro, Astor, Lester, & Benbenishty, 2015). These efforts could be a routine part of data collection when school districts engage in Child Find procedures through community screenings. These data could be compiled over time for the purposes of designing and delivering the most optimal early intervention services with the young military family in mind. Further, school psychologists can contribute to establishing a literature base that tracks military youth over the years, beginning in early childhood when they and their families first form relationships with educators (Cozza et al., 2014). This is an outstanding opportunity for school psychologists to collect much needed developmental information about military youth to better serve them in today's schools. This early childhood application is one example in which the routine practices of school psychologists, such as conducting early childhood screening, could be modified to capture the early childhood screening data of young military children. These efforts, along with the interventions and supports for young military children, could be tracked over time and modified, guided by the data.

The following fictional case study builds upon the introductory content offered in this chapter. Specifically, it describes how a school psychologist could approach this case from a strengths-based/resiliency perspective advocated for working with military youth and their families.

The Calderon family of five comprises Rita (mother, age 43), Tom (father, age 41), and three children (twins, Alicia and Michael, age 10, and Robert, age 3). Rita and Tom, both of Mexican descent, grew up in a midsize town in Texas. Rita is in the Marine Corps Reserve and works as a school secretary. Tom is an accountant in private practice. Alicia and Michael are in the fourth grade at Sunnydale Elementary School that serves a diverse population of students, including a high percentage of youth from Hispanic backgrounds. Alicia and Michael both like their school and teachers a great deal. They are in different classrooms: Alicia has Mr. Mathis and Michael has Ms. Ruben. Alicia plays soccer, while Michael is active in baseball. Robert just started preschool for three mornings a week. Approximately 20% of students at Sunnydale Elementary School are connected with the military, either through the Marine Corps Reserves or through an active-duty military installation located in their town as well.

In terms of early history, Rita and Tom emigrated to the United States as young children with their parents. The maternal grandparents (Emma and Isaac) have remained in the area and live 15 minutes from the Calderon family. They spend significant time with the grandchildren, playing a critical role in child care and attending family events and sports that Alicia and Michael play. Emma and Isaac are most comfortable speaking Spanish. Michael's father, Nathaniel, passed away when Michael was young, and he had significant responsibilities in caring for his three younger siblings. Michael's mother, Maria, lives in California and often spends most of the summer staying with the Calderon family. Rita has had one previous deployment to Iraq when the twins were toddlers. At that time, her mother moved into the home and helped to care for the twins when Tom worked. Her younger sister, Anna, who has two children about the same age as the twins and lives 5 minutes away, provided a great deal of assistance with child care and helping with errands. This was particularly helpful during the tax season, when Tom was gone for long hours and felt that he could not cut back his workload because he is self-employed. Although the family described Rita's previous deployment as highly stressful, they reported being thankful for grandparent support and the support of several childhood friends of Rita's who remained in nearby towns and assisted with the young children on the weekends. Rita has not been called up for active duty and reports that they have all settled into family life. However, recently, Rita received a notice that she was to report for training in a town approximately 2 hours away for an estimated period of 4 months. While Rita and Tom report a close relationship and feel strong family support, they are worried about the separation and how a third young child may create new challenges. Rita's parents, sister, and close friends are willing to help, but Rita and Tom are concerned about relying so much on others who have obligations of their own. Nevertheless, they will be seeking the help of these extended family members and friends. As a school psychologist, how could you assist and provide support to the family? Here are some next steps that the school psychologist could take in implementing a strengths-based/resiliency approach to supporting the Calderon family.

- The school psychologist could conduct an assessment to identify the needs expressed by the family for support related to the upcoming deployment and any family-identified concerns. Using a strengths-based approach, the needs assessment could be developed with guiding questions that facilitate the identification of strengths. The principles of the wraparound planning process—in which family interviews begin from a strengths-based perspective (Bruns et al., 2004, p. 9) and in which needs are determined by the family rather than by clinical diagnostic models aligned with traditional service delivery—could be adopted by the school psychologist. Wraparound planning prioritizes "natural supports" (Bruns et al., 2004, p. 6), such as family and friends, rather than supports tied to traditional social services (Bruns et al., 2004), which is consistent with how the Calderon family defined their support system and how they have problem-solved in the past.

- Taking a strengths-based approach, aligned with models of resiliency, the school psychologist could identify a number of family strengths and natural supports to draw from. The Calderon family has a number of extended family members who have provided support. For instance, Emma and Isaac, the maternal grandparents, as well as Rita's sister, Anna, and family friends have been integral in helping the family in a previous deployment and in their day-to-day lives. These "natural supports" (Bruns et al., 2004, p. 6) were identified by family members as part of a team of individuals already in the family's support system who could assist during Rita's pending deployment.

- Because numerous caretakers are going to be involved with the family and taking on some of the parenting role in Rita's absence, the school psychologist could research and recommend a family-based intervention in close collaboration with the family and close friends. There are a couple of different interventions that have been developed specifically for military families who are experiencing a deployment to select from. One option is the Families OverComing Under Stress (FOCUS) program (Lester et al., 2012, 2013), the school-based version of which has been implemented and evaluated in schools (Garcia et al., 2015). Another option is After Deployment: Adaptive Parenting Tools (ADAPT; Gewirtz, Polusny, Forgatch, DeGarmo, & Marquez, 2009; Gewirtz, 2013; Palmer, 2008). In close collaboration with the family, the school psychologist could review each program's evidence and decide whether the content is culturally responsive and appropriate. The most optimal program is the one selected *with* the family members, not *for* them.

- In this case scenario, the family and school psychologist could perhaps select FOCUS as the primary intervention to implement with Rita, Tom, and the main caregivers to assist during Rita's deployment because of the program's emphasis on strengthening family cohesion, problem solving, and communication for the entire team of caregivers. It is also important in this case to be culturally sensitive to the family in terms of their child-rearing practices as well as in addressing language issues. Therefore, to be culturally responsive, other supplemental materials and exercises should be considered and the program evaluated on an ongoing basis to ensure that it is meeting the Calderon family's needs. For example, the components of the ADAPT program (Gewirtz et al., 2013) specific to relaxation and mindfulness could be embedded in the work with the family and other caregivers. Moreover, throughout Rita's deployment and in the months prior to her return home, a plan with everyone involved could be developed to redistribute parenting tasks upon Rita's return (Esposito-Smythers et al., 2011.

- At the classroom level, the children's teachers could also receive specific psychoeducation about the deployment cycle (Chandra et al., 2011) and consultations with the school psychologist to prevent and address any academic, behavioral, or social–emotional concerns that may arise. The teachers could also serve in a mentorship role with the children, given the positive relationships that already exist.

OVERVIEW OF THE CHAPTERS TO FOLLOW

The subsequent chapters continue to emphasize a strengths-based/resiliency approach (Easterbrooks et al., 2013; Masten, 2011; Park, 2011) grounded in a healthy MTSS foundation (Brown-Chidsey & Andren, 2012). Chapter 2 provides an overview of the various school environments in which military youth are educated to facilitate contextually relevant school psychology service delivery for them and their families. Chapter 3 focuses on how MTSS supports and universal screening efforts can be implemented with this military population, and Chapter 4 describes healthy social development among military youth. Chapter 5 discusses mental health supports with military youth and their families. Chapter 6 covers issues related to school transitions, which tend to be plentiful for military populations. Subsequently, Chapter 7 examines legal considerations, and the culminating Chapter 8 provides an overall summary of the previous chapters and offers some future directions for the field.

Please note that in an attempt to be inclusive of readers who do not identify with masculine or feminine pronouns, the pronouns *they/them/their* are used when referring to a single individual.

CHAPTER 2

Educational Settings Attended by Military Youth
Contextual Considerations and Case Studies

This chapter examines how the varied school contexts and environments in which military youth are educated influence the types of support that may be needed, and considers the factors that are present in these school environments. In particular, issues such as the social supports available for military youth and their families; cultural considerations of the community and country (if the deployment is international); acceptance of military personnel in the community; and the degree of training, resources, expertise, and experience of the school-based professionals are discussed. Fictional "snapshots" of families from these various environments are depicted and the ways in which school psychologists can collaborate with other professionals to meet the needs of military youth and their families based on school context are briefly described. These snapshots are drawn from research on various military installations in the United States and in international military contexts to make the scenarios realistic.

OVERVIEW OF SCHOOL ENVIRONMENTS THAT EDUCATE MILITARY YOUTH

Public Schools/Civilian Settings

Although 80% of school-age children in military families attend public schools (School Superintendents Association, 2019), which are commonly referred to as Civilian schools, there is significant variability in military student enrollment within them. For example, in a given public school, it is possible that a military student may be the only one or one of a few military-connected students, whereas in another public school that is in or near a military installation, there may be large percentages of military students enrolled. It is estimated that there are 160 U.S. public schools housed within military installations (Military One Source, 2018a).

DoD Schools

Other than public schools, military youth may also attend DoD schools, which are run by the U.S. Department of Defense Education Activity (DoDEA) (Military.com, 2019). The DoDEA is a Civilian arm of the DoD (Military.com, 2019). Some DoD school statistics and information include the following:

- According to the DoDEA (2019a), there are 996,069 military-connected children, 73,000 (11.5%) of which attend DoDEA-administered schools across 11 countries, seven states, and two territories.
- DoD schools are found in three regions across the world—(1) DoDEA Americas, (2) DoDEA Europe, and (3) DoDEA Pacific—as well as one available DoDEA Virtual High School (Military One Source, 2018a).
- There are many similarities in policies and practices found in public schools (under the U.S. Department of Education), compared with those operated through the U.S. Department of Defense (e.g., schools under DoDEA).

Non-DoD Schools

A third educational setting for military-connected students is a non-DoD school. Students attend a non-DoD school when the family's military assignment is in an international or overseas country and there is no accessible DoD school. However, the DoDEA runs the non-DoD Schools Program and assists families in locating a school for their dependent child (DoDEA, 2019b). The non-DoD Schools Program office, which is under the jurisdiction of the DoDEA director, reviews the eligibility criteria for dependent children and ultimately approves enrollment of the dependent military student and the necessary support to attend a non-DoD school (DoDEA, 2019b). More information about non-DoD schools is provided in the section on non-DoD schools later in the chapter.

PUBLIC SCHOOLS/CIVILIAN SETTINGS

The fact that most military youth attend Civilian public schools (Clever & Segal, 2013; School Superintendents Association, 2019) has led to an increased awareness of the presence of military youth in all settings, including public ones, through campaigns across the country such as the Purple Up Campaign (DoDEA, 2019a). School psychologists can expand this awareness in their respective schools and communities. They play a valuable role in identifying and supporting military youth in all educational settings, but particularly in Civilian ones that are not necessarily organized to meet the needs of military youth as DoD-operated schools are. For instance, it is entirely possible that teachers working in Civilian settings may not even be aware that military youth are among their students (Military Child Education Coalition/Columbia University Center for Public Research and Leadership, 2017).

Awareness of Public School Military Students and Use of Military Student Identifiers

Recent legislation under the Every Student Succeeds Act (ESSA; described in Chapter 7) may help to increase educator awareness about the presence of military students in public schools and how best to support their academic, behavioral, and social–emotional success. Unlike military-connected students in DoD or non-DoD schools in international settings, the connection that students have to the military and the potential harm caused by military-related life stressors, such as an upcoming deployment or a military move, may not be as apparent to public school educators. In 2015, after a great deal of legislative and advocacy work on the part of many organizations that cherish military families, like the Military Child Education Coalition (MCEC), the ESSA now mandates that states identify students who have an active-duty military parent through the use of a military student identifier (Mesecar & Soifer, 2018; Military Child Education Coalition/Columbia University Center for Public Research and Leadership, 2017). As expanded on in Chapter 7, although military student identifier data are collected for students whose parents are in active duty, not every student impacted by family military service is accounted for through the ESSA military subgroup reporting requirements. Military service members in the National Guard and Reserves are not classified as full-time National Guard Duty members and therefore are not covered by ESSA regulations. As a result, this particular subgroup of students may not even be acknowledged as connected with the military and will most likely attend Civilian schools, where they are least likely to be identified, and therefore, honored and supported. Despite strong advocacy efforts of the MCEC to include children of all military personnel in the National Guard and Reserves, the ESSA has fallen short by excluding children of this service group (Muller, Tong, & Irby, 2016). Building upon what has been started through the ESSA military student identifier, school psychologists and other school-based mental health professionals who work in public Civilian schools can advocate for more inclusive collection of military student data than is minimally required under the ESSA. Affirmative communication to counselors and teachers about military identifier data and whether there are military students in one's classroom does not happen as a matter of course (Military Child Education Coalition/Columbia University Center for Public Research and Leadership, 2017). It presents an opportunity for school psychologists to weigh in to ensure that these data are shared with teachers and other school personnel who need the information to properly educate all military-connected students. School psychologists can also compensate for the limitations of ESSA data collection with National Guards/Reserve military personnel by collecting their own, more military-inclusive data and by being visible in the school, so that all students and families know who they are and are comfortable seeking them out as needed. One particular area in which school psychologists could assist military youth is through facilitating social supports, which will vary according to the type of school—for example, DoD versus public Civilian schools—that military youth attend. School context matters greatly in thinking about the extent of supports that may be required, given that there is a significant variation in the attendance rates of military youth, for example, in a DoD versus a Civilian school, where there may be only a few military-connected students.

Social Support of Military Students in Public School Environments

Beyond utilizing the ESSA-mandated military student identifier to simply determine which students in a district are connected with the military and how to use these data more effectively, another important area of concern is understanding the social structures and supports available to military youth. This issue is particularly relevant for military youth who attend Civilian public schools, because the size of their military-connected peer group is quite variable. Receiving support from and making connections with peers are important for all students, and may be particularly critical for military youth. For example, Bradshaw, Sudhinaraset, Mmari and Blum (2010) found that adolescents described their peer social connections as stronger compared to their connections with adult educators. Having other peers from the military to connect with and a welcoming social environment across developmental stages is the main topic of Chapter 4 and is not the focus of this chapter. Simply put, school districts have a responsibility to make everyone feel welcome and at ease socially. School psychologists play a major role in establishing welcoming social environments and in facilitating connections among students, and using data to evaluate these efforts are important. The shape that these efforts take will depend on the school context, with particular attention paid to the number of military youth enrolled; whether the school is a DoD, Civilian public, or international one; and other student and community demographics. An overarching question is whether military students perceive that they are socially supported and accepted or whether they experience isolation. Although military students have different individual needs, if they do not have the opportunity to interact with other military student peers, they may perceive that their peers do not understand them. Transitioning to and from schools, regardless of whether the school is a Civilian public one, a DoD school, an international or a private school, is a challenge that military families face at high rates, as described throughout this book. As earlier noted, military youth who transition to Civilian public schools may have a higher probability of encountering school personnel and students who are unfamiliar with their needs and how to support them. Table 2.1 provides some specific guiding questions for Civilian public schools as they consider how to best support military youth based on the demographic characteristics of their local school context and community. The responses to the guiding questions depend on whether a school setting has a low or high percentage of military youth. The guiding questions can help schools consider

TABLE 2.1. Guiding Questions for Public Schools

Guiding question	Low presence of military youth	High presence of military youth
What percentage of your public school and/or district enrollment comprises military-connected students?	Consider setting up a program such as the Student2Student program developed by the Military Child Education Coalition (2019a) among military and Civilian students, described at *www.militarychild.org/audience/students*	Find opportunities to pair military students with one another through having groups for military students that serve a social support function.
What training have your public school teachers, administrators, and other school professionals had with respect to military-connected students and their culture?	It is apparent that training about military students and how to support them should be integrated into professional development and revisited on an ongoing basis. There are many available resources for professional educators, which have been described elsewhere, in a variety of formats. See the Military Child Education Coalition (2019b) website at *www.militarychild.org/audience/professionals*	Ongoing training and revisiting professional development remain important. In the last few years, there have been several key developments and innovations in supporting military students, particularly the ESSA-required military student identifier. There is a growing effort to more effectively use these data in a more comprehensive manner. Determine whether there is a school liaison assigned to your students' military installation, which is more likely where there are high concentrations of military youth. If so, seek out their help and access the following URL for further information: *https://branchta.org/role-school-liaison-officer-slo* (Military Parent Technical Assistance Center, 2017).
What supports are available for military families, and how does the school communicate with them?	Seek out military families to serve as leaders who can let schools know what is helpful for them. Work with military liaisons and school-based mental health professionals in this process. Continue to support families in identifying what is helpful and make changes based on military family feedback and support.	Continue to monitor supports and collaboration with families. Ensure that military families have a voice in determining the supports they need. Seek military family input frequently and continue to make adjustments as needed.
What collaboration, if any, exists with the military installation in the school?	Seek out input from and form collaborative partnerships with military families in the community. If there is not an identified military school liaison, which may be the case in communities where there is not a military installation, seek assistance by accessing one of the organizations specializing in supporting the education of military youth.	Seek out input from and collaborate with military families and ensure that they have a voice in determining what is helpful for them. Again, determine whether your school has a school liaison officer and, if so, seek out this person.

areas of focus and points of intervention for ensuring that military students have access to adequate social supports.

Local Context and Community Cultural Considerations

Military-connected students who navigate across public school environments may encounter students and staff who lack an awareness of military culture or even the knowledge that they are military youth. Military children transition among schools between six and nine times during the school years spanning kindergarten through high school (Astor, 2011, as cited in Ruff & Keim, 2014). This means that, on average, these students will enter a new school with its own context and understanding of military culture every year or every other year. Each school, district, and community has its own culture that military-connected children are introduced to each time they move. Military youth must navigate these school cultures, frequently on their own if school staff are not adequately aware of military culture and trained to facilitate a transition. As just a few examples, schools differ in size; whether they are urban, suburban, or rural; the racial and ethnic demographics of the student and staff population; the level of community affluence; and the policies and guidelines of the state education agency that oversees school districts; among many other factors. We consider a fictional snapshot of a family in a public school environment that features school transitions to illustrate how the population and demographics, particularly the military demographics of the schools, affect the family and how a school psychologist could respond.

Fictional Family Snapshot in a Public School Environment

The Brown family comprises Stacey (mother), who is an active-duty member of the Air Force; William (father), who is in the Army reserves; and twins Brad and Nicole (15). Their racial and ethnic identity is White. The family has moved five times since Brad and Nicole have started kindergarten and are now planning a sixth move over the summer. Now going into their senior year of high school, the twins are moving from the Seattle/Tacoma Washington area to near Bedford, Massachusetts, where Stacey has an assignment in a small Air Force base. The family plans to move to off-base housing and to enroll the twins in the local public school district. The concentration of military families in the area is much lower than where they lived in the Tacoma/Seattle area, which has a high concentration of Army and Air Force personnel and a public school that serves a high percentage of military youth. The new high school, which is much smaller and enrolls a very small percentage of military youth, will be a huge change for Brad and Nicole. Invoking the Military Interstate Children's Compact, the receiving and sending counselors can discuss course placement and graduation requirements. (More information about the Military Interstate Children's Compact is presented in Chapters 6 and 7.) Having a welcoming school staff member at the receiving school, such as a school-based psychologist or counselor who is familiar with the Compact, can help in resolving some issues involved in the transition to a smaller high school. Brad and Nicole fulfilled a number of state requirements in civics and history that could potentially be transferrable. Since the required math curriculum varies by state, a review of the content already covered could help to determine the appropriate requirements for their final year of mathematics. In addition, Brad and Nicole have both taken advanced mathematics and want to pursue a career in engineering and are applying to the United States Air Force Academy. The school psychologist plans to work with the school counselor to ensure that Brad and Nicole are placed in the proper mathematics courses, including reaching out to a local college to facilitate their enrollment in courses beyond the high school math curriculum. During this critical time for the twins, the school psychologist can additionally be helpful by connecting the family with other military families in the area if they so desire. They can also reach out to the school liaisons in the sending and the receiving schools (if they are available) to seek out additional information and to set up a consultation.

DoD SCHOOLS

Accreditation

The estimated 996,069 military-connected students who attend DoD schools may live in one of three regions across the world described earlier or attend a "virtual high school" (DoDEA, 2019a). There is a great deal of practical information on the DoDEA general website and on specific pages about how DoDEA schools are organized and structured; where they are located; their curriculum and graduation requirements; and their accreditation reports. DoD schools are all accredited on a 5-year cycle by AdvancED, which is the parent company for the following three U.S.-based accrediting agencies: (1) North Central Association Commission on Accreditation and School Improvement (NCA CASI); (2) Northwest Accreditation Commission (NWAC); and (3) the Southern Association of Colleges and Schools Council on Accreditation and School Improvement (SACS CASI) (DoDEA, 2019c). As stated within a "frequently asked questions" document on the DoDEA web page, DoD accreditation is sought so that students can more easily transfer credits when switching schools and have access to federal loans and post-secondary and military opportunities that require graduation from an accredited school (DoDEA, 2019d).

In comparison, the U.S. Department of Education (DoE), which oversees U. S. public schools that receive federal funding, does not accredit or recognize agencies that accredit public and private elementary and secondary schools (DoE, 2009). However, most state education agencies, which have oversight over education for each state, require or advocate for their school districts to be accredited (DoE, International Affairs Office, 2007). Schools that are recognized by their state education agency through their approval process, either through accreditation or another state-driven process, are recognized schools in the U.S. education system (DoE, International Affairs Office, 2007). States also recognize U.S. private schools that undergo accreditation through the DoD, the Department of Homeland Security, and relevant state agencies (DoE, International Affairs Office, 2007).

Table 2.2 summarizes the information offered on the various DoDEA websites, with accompanying URLs. School psychologists can share this information and website addresses with military families who may be transitioning within and across the DoDEA school system.

Graduation Requirements

The DoDEA has now recognized the Military Interstate Children's Compact Commission (MIC3, 2018), known as "The Compact" for high schools (DoDEA, 2019g). More detailed

TABLE 2.2. Web Resources for DoD Schools

Website descriptor	Website address	Summary of major content
DoDEA main website	*www.dodea.edu* (DoDEA, 2019a)	The main page for the DoDEA website contains substantive information about the organization, curriculum, and graduation requirements of DoD schools.
Listing of DoDEA school Accreditation Reports System (DARS)	*https://webapps.dodea.edu/ DARS/Home.cfm* (DoDEA, 2019e)	This site contains the external AdvancED reports, which are publicly available and can be searched by school.
College and Career Ready Standards (CCR)	*www.ed.gov/k-12reforms/ standards#page-header* (DoDEA, 2019f)	The DoDEA has adopted CCR, as have most U.S. states (DoE, n.d). This has been done to ensure high-quality standards and continuity with other educational settings within and outside of DoDEA-run schools (DoDEA, 2019f).
Curricular requirements	*www.dodea.edu/Curriculum/ index.cfm* (DoDEA, 2019g)	This DoDEA web page contains curricular information organized by program type (e.g., Language Arts, Math, Gifted Education, Special Education, English Language Learners, and Physical Education). Course descriptions are also provided. Contact information for an identified person supporting each curricular subtype (DoDEA, 2019g) is also given.
Graduation requirements	*www.dodea.edu/ collegeCareerReady/ graduation-requirements.cfm* (DoDEA, 2019h)	The course and graduation requirements are clearly specified on the DoDEA website, (DoDEA, 2019h). There is also a planning document example at *www.dodea.edu/students/ upload/4Year-Plan_Example-1.pdf* (DoDEA, 2019p)
		Counselors and students can complete the plan together to pursue various post-high school options (e.g., 2-year and 4-year college or university or entry to a branch of the military; DoDEA, 2019g).

information is provided in Chapters 6 (specifically on transition issues) and in Chapter 7 (on legal matters) about the Compact. Stated briefly, the Compact has been adopted by all 50 states, although the statute language varies by state. The purpose of the Compact is to provide some accommodations to help military youth as they relocate often across state lines from one school district to another district that has different curriculum and graduation requirements. Agreements exist for both the sending and receiving districts with respect to: (1) enrollment, (2), course/program placement, (3) attendance, (4) eligibility, and (5) graduation accommodations (Fenning et al., 2013).

Academic Achievement in DoD Schools

The academic achievement of military-connected students attending DoD schools is stronger relative to students who attend regular public schools, based on the 2017 National Assessment of Educational Progress (NAEP) data (Towhey, 2018) as well as the most recently available NAEP math (NAEP, 2019a) and NAEP reading assessments (2019b). Some key NAEP findings are as follows:

• Based on the NAEP administered in 2017, fourth graders attending DoDEA schools had the second highest reading score in the nation (DoDEA, 2018; NAEP, 2018a, as cited in Towhey, 2018) and were tied with one state (Massachusetts) in mathematics (NAEP, 2018b, as cited in Towhey, 2018). In the most recently available 2019 NAEP assessments, 4th graders attending DoDEA schools scored highest in the nation in both reading (NAEP, 2019a, as cited in DoDEA, 2019n) and math (NAEP, 2019b, as cited in DoDEA, 2019o).

• According to the 2017 NAEP findings, DoDEA eighth graders earned the highest reading scores in the nation (DoDEA, 2018; NAEP, 2018a, as cited in Towhey, 2018) and remained well above the national average for mathematics, reflecting a slight increase from 2015 (DoDEA, 2018; NAEP, 2018b, as cited in Towhey, 2018). 2019 findings show a similarly strong performance from eighth graders, who came in first place in reading (NAEP, 2019a, as cited in DoDEA, 2019n) and second in math (NAEP, 2019b, as cited in DoDEA, 2019o).

• Black and Latinx students attending DoDEA schools had the highest scores on the 2019 NAEP, compared with students in their same racial/ethnic groups attending non-DoDEA schools (DoDEA, 2019o). These findings suggest that the "education debt," as coined by Gloria Ladson-Billings (Ladson-Billings, 2006), rather than the "achievement gap" often used when considering historically minoritized students, is smaller in DoDEA schools compared with Civilian public schools

• NAEP findings in previous years are consistent with the two most recent 2017 and 2019 NAEP findings (NAEP, 2018a; NAEP, 2018b; NAEP, 2019a; NAEP, 2019b). Specifically, military students attending DoDEA schools have consistently shown stronger academic performance in the aggregate, and disaggregated by race and ethnicity when compared with peers attending public/Civilian schools (Smrekar & Owens, 2003). Based on earlier 1998 NAEP data collected with military youth in DoDEA schools, organized at that time as DoD Dependents Schools (DoDDS) in overseas military installations and DoD Domestic Dependent Elementary and Secondary Schools (DDESS) in the United States (Smrekar & Owens, 2003), youth in DDESS schools were second in the nation, whereas those in DoDDS schools were fourth in the nation in writing. In the area of reading, only two states had a higher percentage of students at the level of proficiency compared with DoDDS and DDESS schools (Smrekar & Owens, 2003).

- When looking at these data disaggregated by race and ethnicity, Black and Latinx students in DoDEA-run schools were first or second relative to their peers in non-DoDEA schools (Smrekar & Owens, 2003). Although writing opportunity gaps existed in that White students scored higher than Latinx and Black students and White students scored higher than Black students in reading, the opportunity gaps were much narrower in DoDEA schools in looking at these earlier data (Ladson-Billings, 2006). Moreover, all DoDEA racial and ethnic groups' average reading and writing scores exceeded the national average (Smrekar & Owens, 2003).

Characteristics of DoD Schools

The characteristics of DoDEA schools that may contribute to the academic success of their students, particularly the consistent findings showing that racial and ethnic minority students have stronger academic achievement in DoDEA schools compared with their peers who hold the same racial/ethnic identities attending public schools, have been explored (Bridglall & Gordon, 2003; Smrekar & Owens, 2003). These characteristics include their high, rigorous academic standards and being part of a military culture that values discipline, training, and an emphasis on education (Bridglall & Gordon, 2003, Smrekar & Owens, 2003). Furthermore, the community aspect of DoDEA schools, facilitated by being located in military installations, may foster better communication, shared values, and a commitment to the school community (Bridglall & Gordon, 2003).

In addition, DoDEA teachers often stay in their jobs for many years and therefore are experienced in working with military youth who face multiple school transitions (Smrekar & Owens, 2003). Teachers in DoDEA schools also have access to high-quality professional development (Bridglall & Gordon, 2003). An additional feature of DoDEA schools viewed as contributing to academic success are teacher and staff access to data that inform curricular decisions (Bridglall & Gordon, 2003). Advantages in resources, financial and otherwise, are also seen as critical, such as the amount of money spent per pupil (Bridglall & Gordon, 2003; Smrekar & Owens, 2003). As an example of a personnel resource, DoDEA schools have historically employed guidance counselors whose primary role is to welcome incoming students, and records clerks whose responsibility is the efficient transfer of records (Smreker & Owens, 2003). DoDEA schools are also, on the average, smaller than their public school counterparts (Bridglall& Gordon, 2003; Smrekar & Owens, 2003) and therefore have an advantage of being able to provide individualized attention to students.

School-based personnel, including school mental health professionals who work in all types of schools that support military-connected students, can integrate the findings about successful DoDEA schools into their work. When working with military youth in Civilian schools, for example, school psychologists can advocate for more personnel to help with the efficient transfer of records. They can also advocate for the increasing use of data, using already available academic records, or ensure that additional screening data be collected in the absence of this information. School psychologists can also ensure that their schools are welcoming environments that encourage inclusiveness for military youth, particularly those who may not have natural supports or are currently being educated with other military youth.

We next turn to a fictional snapshot of a case scenario in a DoD school.

Fictional Family Snapshot in a DoD School

The members of the Ross family include Sam (father, 48) and Irene (mother, 50). Sarah (daughter, 13), and Ryan (son, 21). Sarah has Down syndrome and has had an individualized education plan (IEP) since preschool in early childhood. She is very independent and has strong verbal skills. She has often been included in general education classes, but there has been some variability depending on the schools she has attended. Her parents often need to advocate for her to be placed in the appropriate classes and not be immediately placed in self-contained special education classes. Ryan is nearing completion of his undergraduate degree in aerospace engineering at the Air Force Academy in Colorado. He would like to serve as an officer in the military once he finishes his degree. Sam is a career military officer in the Air Force and is currently deployed in Germany. Sam is likely to have a 2-year overseas deployment, but it is uncertain. Irene serves in the Army Reserves and is not currently on active duty. She is an accountant by training and does some consulting work out of her home office. She also serves as a special education advocate for other families. The family has moved seven times, but for the most part have lived in the Southeast, and the children have attended DoDEA schools. The family currently lives on an Air Force military installation in Georgia. Sarah is transitioning to a local high school and not to the DoDEA school in their community. Her family is working with both the DoDEA personnel at her middle school and the high school personnel who are reviewing her IEP and helping with course placements. The special education evaluation was recently completed at the DoDEA school. However, the incoming school has not historically educated students with intellectual disabilities to their full potential in general education. The family is advocating for full inclusion in most courses with push-in supports. The accepting school has voiced concerns about this request, but the family has advocated that Sarah be enrolled with her current IEP, which is part of the provisions of the Military Interstate Children's Compact. The incoming school is accepting the IEP and the family's request for a meeting to be held after the first quarter of high school to evaluate how Sarah is doing and to make any adjustments. This fictional case study illustrates the need for all school personnel to be familiar with the Military Interstate Children's Compact and to hear the concerns voiced by these families with an open mind. The case study also reminds us of the importance of collaboration and communication between the school psychologists in the sending and the receiving schools in the best interest of military students. Collaborating with one another and the family provides a smooth transition and ensures that the family and Sarah are heard in terms of their hopes and dreams for their child's future education.

NON-DoD SCHOOLS

When military families relocate to overseas locations where an accessible DoD school does not exist, funding for their education may be provided by the military through the Non-DoD Schools Program (NDSP). According to information provided by DoDEA, which manages the NDSP (DoDEA, 2019i), the following conditions must be met for approval of a dependent child of a military "sponsor" (the parent) to attend a non-DoD school: (1) the sponsor must have a military assignment and live in a location that is out of the commuting reach of a DoD school, (2) the dependent must also be authorized by the military to reside with the parent at the assignment location, (3) the sponsor must be on active duty and stationed overseas with specific orders called "permanent change of station" or qualify as a Civilian DoD full-time employee stationed overseas and be a national/U.S. citizen, (4) the sponsor must have military authorization to transport the dependent child overseas at government expense, and (5) the sponsor must receive a monetary allowance for housing that is at the family or dependent rate. The Non-DoD Schools Program Orientation (DoDEA, 2019i) is a resource that provides detailed information about enrollment procedures and policies related to military coverage of educational expenses, and the reader is directed to this document for further information. There are a number of non-DoD educational options; they include: (1) local public schools; (2) local private day schools; (3) local non-English-speaking schools; (4) boarding schools; and (5) home study, private instruction, or virtual education (DoDEA, 2019i). Each of these school options has specific requirements that need to be followed for approved educational funding, such as tuition, transportation costs, and other educational expenses. Although the DoDEA does not endorse or certify schools, families are allowed to make a selection from among authorized options, with the priority being the choice of a school that will facilitate transition back to a U.S. school (DoDEA, 2019i). There are a number of resources that are helpful for parents in selecting schools, and include a list of non-DoD schools (DoDEA, 2019j), a guidance document for selecting an international school (DoDEA, 2019k) and non-English school guidance (DoDEA, 2019l). In addition, for parents electing home study or private instruction that may or may not incorporate virtual learning, the DoDEA Program Orientation document provides a link to the home study education plan that can be completed by the family (DoDEA, 2019m). Table 2.3 contains the web address for and a short summary description of each of these resources.

The DoDEA Program orientation document also contains information about the maximum allowable expenses that the military will provide for a dependent child's education

TABLE 2.3. Web Resources for Non-DoD Schools

Website descriptor	Website address	Summary of major content
Non-DoD Schools Program Orientation	*https://content.dodea.edu/teach_learn/partnership/ndsp/ndsp_orientation/index.html*	This 22-page document provides comprehensive information for families considering transitioning to a non-DoD overseas location and school placement. Topics include eligibility requirements, educational allowances, determining whether the post is a non-DoD location, annual registration, withdrawal, considerations for dependents with special needs, etc. (DoDEA, 2019i).
List of non-DoD schools	*www.dodea.edu/nonDoD/resources/locatingschools.cfm*	This website contains a link to an Excel spreadsheet listing non-DoD schools by location (separated by tab). Within the tab, one can view whether the instruction is in English and whether the institution is a boarding school (DoDEA, 2019j).
Guidance document for selecting an international school	*www.dodea.edu/nonDoD/upload/choosinginternationalschools.pdf*	This four-page document has helpful guiding questions for families to consider when selecting an international school, such as questions about the individual student; the curriculum; school structure and facilities; the staff; and about logistics regarding funding, reimbursement, and travel distances (DoDEA, 2019k).
Non-English school guidance	*www.dodea.edu/nonDoD/upload/NonEnglishSchoolGuidance.pdf*	This is a helpful one-page resource for families who are considering a school that offers instruction in a language other than English. The developmental age of the child is highlighted as a consideration, as well as reimbursement issues and consultations with the NDSP Educational Specialist (DoDEA, 2019l).
Home Study Education Plan	*www.dodea.edu/nonDoD/upload/NDSP-Home-Study-Education-Plan-Revised-30-Jan-2020.pdf*	This is a form that families complete when implementing a home study plan under the auspices of a non-DoD school. Families provide information about which home-based education curriculum they are using and whether it meets the requirements of the state they designate. The form also lists resources for service members to access (i.e., library and language resources) (DoDEA, 2019m).

that can help families decide which non-DoD educational option is best for their child. The Department of State Standardized Regulations (DSSR) Educational allowance is a rate set by grade level and is based on whether the military assignment is "at post" or "away from post" (DoDEA, 2019i). In addition, there are "one time" fee coverages that are not part of the DSSR expenses and are paid once per tour (DoDEA, 2019i). Families with children who have special education needs coordinate and receive approval of all services by working with a non-DoDEA educational specialist (DoDEA, 2019i). Students with special education needs have a different rate than what is specified as the standard DSSR at-post and away-from-post rates (DoDEA, 2019i). In addition, there are allowable expenses for special instruction, such as needed tutoring, and coverage of required U.S. school system courses or gifted education may additionally be authorized as supplementary expenses (DoDEA, 2019i).

When making an international move and selecting a non-DoD school, families should work with their specific NDSP Liaison and School Liaison Officer. For children who have or are thought to have special education needs, the non-DoDEA educational specialist is a critical partner (DoDEA, 2019i). The posted up-to-date resources on the DoDEA website for non-DoDEA schools contained in Table 2.3 are excellent. In collaboration with a school professional, such as their school psychologist, families should access these valuable and comprehensive resources on a regular basis, but be aware that they can change frequently, particularly the DSSR rates and international school options (DoDEA, 2019i). School psychologists and other school-based mental health professionals who work with military families, either stateside or in international settings, can help support them in making the most optimal school decision for their children by carefully considering their educational priorities. School professionals can also help families make optimal decisions by helping them research non-DoD school options that will facilitate a successful reentry back to the United States.

When families are relocating from a non-DoD overseas post back to the United States, school psychologists and other mental health professionals can help by ensuring that they are informed about the relevant components of the Interstate Military Children's Compact (Council of State Governments, 2013) so they can advocate for a successful educational transition.

A fictional snapshot of a family who is relocating as part of the mother's overseas military assignment is depicted next.

Fictional Family Snapshot in a Non-DoD-Administered School

The Marks family consists of Danielle (mother), David (father), and 5-year-old twins Sam (son) and Alyse (daughter). The twins' birthday is August 15, so they just made the cutoff to start kindergarten in Columbus, Georgia, where Danielle is assigned as a military officer in the U.S. Army. The children attend the local public school that has a high percentage of military families and provides ongoing programs and supports, such as parent meetings specifically for military families. Danielle's main role in the army installation is to provide military training to new recruits. David taught elementary school for 10 years, but once the children were born, he became a stay-at-home parent and is a substitute teacher.

Danielle has just received an international assignment to Belgium, which is anticipated to take place in December. This deployment is expected to be at least 6 months, but perhaps longer. The entire family would like to travel to Brussels, Belgium, so they will be together and the children will have an international experience. Danielle and David see this transition as an opportunity for their children to learn French when they are relatively young, which they view as an optimal time for both children to be exposed to a foreign language. It is now October, so the family has a short window of time to plan the move and transition their children to a new school.

As Danielle and David plan their move, they are working with their children's current kindergarten teachers, school psychologists, and the school social worker to find the most optimal early primary school setting. They review the results of early literacy screening done in the fall, and note that both children are meeting expected benchmarks. They also review the document "Non-English School Guidance," posted on the DoDEA website (DoDEA, 2019l) and consider its recommendations. In particular, the parents weigh the importance of acquiring foundational early literacy skills in English when the family ultimately relocates back to the United States. Therefore, they pursue private accredited international school options that provide instruction in English, are located in Brussels, and are within driving distance of the military housing the family will live in. The parents decide that they will obtain some supplemental instruction in French through enrichment courses. They begin filling out the registration paperwork and obtain needed documentation from the children's current school in which they started kindergarten. They check the DSSR allowance and confirm that expenses for transportation, tuition, and other fees are covered, so they can budget for additional expenses they will incur, such as the planned French language courses. They and their current teachers and school-based mental health support staff review the document "Choosing an International School," also posted on the DoDEA website (DoDEA, 2019k) to further refine their selection. Ultimately, they review the spreadsheet of NDSP schools (DoDEA, 2019j), and find a school that fits their priorities for English-only instruction and accessibility to the military installation. The school they select is also accredited by the Council of International Schools. They work with their school's professional staff to review and begin filling out the paperwork for approval of their desired school. They contact their NDSP Liaison for further clarification of the policies and procedures for obtaining approval for their children to enroll in the school they have chosen. At the end of the process, they are excited about their international journey and are comfortable with their decision.

CONCLUSION

Children connected with the military have a variety of school options. Most attend Civilian public schools (School Superintendents Association, 2019), but they may also attend DoD and non-DoD schools. These educational environments vary significantly in terms of how they are administered, the percentage of military children they enroll, and whether they are housed in the United States or overseas. School psychologists and other school-based mental health professionals can be instrumental partners to military families as they navigate the waters of school transitions with each military-related move. Making a decision about a school for a child is one of the most important decisions parents can make. School psychologists, given their training in data-based decision making, mental health, and counseling, can serve an invaluable function at these critical junctures for military youth and their families.

CHAPTER 3

Universal Screening Data and Multi-Tiered Systems of Support for Military Children

GENERAL PRINCIPLES OF MTSS

As introduced in Chapter 1, MTSS (commonly referred to historically as *response to intervention*) are models of service delivery that are increasingly being conceptualized, implemented, and evaluated mostly by school psychologists in individual public schools and districts and at a broader statewide level (Castillo & Batsche, 2012; McIntosh & Goodman, 2016; State of Florida's MTSS, 2012). MTSS are also school-based public health policy models that closely align with the recommendations of military researchers for a public health approach that focuses on the collection of normative universal school-based developmental data about military youth, rather than an approach that solely focuses on data measuring individual psychopathology (Burns & Gibbons, 2012; Cozza et al., 2014; Garcia et al., 2015; Gilreath et al., 2014; Stoiber, 2014).

MTSS are integrated models that provide support both in traditional academic domains and in behavioral and social–emotional domains (State of Florida's MTSS, 2012; Stoiber, 2014), given that students with academic problems often have behavioral problems as well (Algozzine, Wang, & Violette, 2011; National Association of School Psychologists [NASP], 2009a, 2009b). The integrated nature of MTSS provides an opportunity for school teams to consider behavioral and academic issues concurrently and not in isolation (Lane, Oakes, Carter, & Messenger, 2015; McIntosh, Flannery, Sugai, Braun, & Cochrane, 2008). Within MTSS, school teams determine, through the use of data, which academic, behavioral, and social–emotional supports and interventions will be delivered, evaluated, and potentially modified within a continuum of tiered instructional support and with which students. MTSS conceptualization begins with supports delivered to all students (universal/Tier 1), followed by the provision of supplemental/group (secondary/Tier 2) and/or implementation of the most intensive individualized programming and instruction for a small percentage of students who need the most support (tertiary/Tier 3) (Brown-Chidsey & Andren, 2013; Burns & Gibbons, 2012; McIntosh & Goodman, 2016). A variety of problem-solving models are available to school psychologists, including those with origins in problem-solving consultation that can readily be adapted for use by multi-tiered problem-solving teams that school psychologists often lead (Kratochwill, Altschaefl & Bice-Urbach, 2014).

UNIVERSAL SCREENING AS A MAJOR MTSS PRACTICE

A hallmark of MTSS models is the universal screening of the entire school population through the use of efficient and standard formative assessment tools tied to educational outcomes, which is conducted periodically during set times (McIntosh & Goodman, 2016; State of Florida's MTSS, 2012). Universal screening of student performance on indicators tied to expected academic, behavioral, and social–emotional outcomes helps the school team assess how school practices are working for the entire student population and identify as early as possible students who may need additional support beyond universal/Tier 1 supports (Albers & Kettler, 2014; Intervention Central, n.d.).

Academic Screening

Within the academic domain, most school psychologists will be familiar with the MTSS data-based components of academic screening and progress monitoring, through the use of formative assessment tools. CBMs (Deno, 1985; Shinn, 2010, 2013) are the most common formative measures aligned with MTSS that can serve as both universal screeners and progress monitoring tools (Shinn, 2013). As progress monitoring tools, CBMs are very sensitive to small changes in student performance as part of an intervention and/or instructional adjustments (Shinn, 2013). Therefore, CBMs provide an efficient way for teams to evaluate their core and/or supplemental instruction with students and allow them to quickly make adjustments as needed (Shinn, 2010). Over many years, formative assessment, through the use of CBMs, has advanced greatly. The recent literature has not questioned whether formative assessment and CBMs should be used at all, merely how frequently such data should be collected to balance efficiency with maximum benefit for students (Jenkins, Schulze, Marti, & Harbaugh, 2017).

Behavioral/Social–Emotional Screening

In addition to examining extant school behavioral data, such as office discipline referrals (ODRs; McIntosh et al. 2010), behavioral and social–emotional rating scales can serve as universal screeners, early identification measures, and progress monitoring tools (Albers & Ketter, 2014; Dever, Kamphaus, Dowdy, Raines, & DiStefano, 2013; Dowdy, Doane, Eklund, & Dever, 2011; Lane et al., 2011; University of Missouri Evidence-Based Intervention Network, 2015). A comprehensive review of research-based universal behavioral and academic screeners is beyond the scope of this chapter. Consider consulting the following two websites compiled by researchers who are conducting comprehensive reviews of these screeners and performing a service for those in practice: (1) the Comprehensive Integrated Three-Tiered Model of Prevention (Ci3T) at *www.ci3t.org/screening* (Ci3T, 2019) and (2) the University of Missouri Evidence-Based Intervention (EBI) group (University of Missouri Evidence-Based Intervention Network, 2015). The Ci3T (2019) website provides comprehensive information about several universal behavioral and/or social–emotional screeners, including those that can be used with groups that range from young children to young adults. The measures described on the Ci3T website include (1) the Behavioral and Emotional Screening System (BASC-3 BESS; Kamphaus & Reynolds, 2007); (2) the Student Risk Screening Scale—Internalizing and Externalizing (adapted from Drummond, 1994; Lane & Menzies, 2009); (3) the Student Risk Screening Scale for Early Childhood (Lane et al., 2015); (4) the Strengths and Difficulties Questionnaire (SDQ; Goodman, 1997); (5) the Systematic Screening for Behavior Disorders (Walker, Severson, & Feil, 2014); and (6) the Social, Academic, and Emotional Behavior Risk Screener (SAEBRS; Kilgus, Chafouleas, & Riley-Tillman, 2013). In reviewing this comprehensive website, school psychologists can select from a suite of behavioral and social emotional screening tools that can be used to screen all students in a school, which, by definition, would include military-connected youth. It should also be noted that some of the tools and measures are accessible for free, along with cut scores on the Ci3T website, and include the Student Risk Screening Scale for Early Childhood (Lane et al., 2015) and the Student Risk Screening Scale—Internalizing and Externalizing (Lane & Menzes, 2009); other measures are available for a fee (Ci3T, 2019).

The University of Missouri EBI group (University of Missouri Evidence-Based Intervention Network, 2015) has also compiled, summarized, and evaluated a number of research-validated screening measures. These measures overlap with several on the Ci3T website and include the SAEBRS (Kilgus, Chafouleas, & Riley-Tillman, 2013) and the BASC3 BESS (Kamphaus & Reynolds, 2007). The University of Missouri EBI website provides a brief summary of the reviewed screening tools, including information about a tool's reliability/validity, administration procedures, and the overall strengths and weaknesses of each measure. School psychologists should investigate the tools and measures on these websites to determine what best suits their purpose and local context.

APPLICATION OF DECISION RULES

Another key hallmark of MTSS is the use of universal screening data to support teams in making decision rules about how effective the tiered supports are in the school setting overall and when students should be transitioned across tiers of support to receive the most appropriate instructional adjustments. Universal decisions are often based on the percentage of youth in a school population that meet or do not meet established district academic, behavioral, and social–emotional benchmarks (Stoiber, 2014). A major focus of school teams is to ensure that universal/Tier 1 supports are as effective as possible and founded on scientifically-based practices (Cusumano, Algozzine, & Algozzine, 2014). With a strong foundation of Tier 1 supports (e.g., core instruction), the maximum percentage of students possible within a school will meet established grade-level expectations without requiring more labor-intensive instructional supports (State of Florida's MTSS, 2012). In addition, even students not meeting universal screening benchmarks may still benefit from receiving Tier 1 scientifically-based instruction in combination with Tier 2 supports (Stevens, Vaughn, Swanson, & Scammacca, 2020). Decision rules apply to these students to determine whether they should receive targeted Tier 2 supports and/or more intensive, individualized Tier 3 supports.

Within the behavioral and social–emotional realm, when systemwide behavioral and social–emotional supports are in place at full fidelity (e.g., analogous to universal/Tier 1), then implementation of supports with students who need targeted/Tier 2 and/or individualized/Tier 3 are more effective, particularly at the Tier 2 level (Kim, McIntosh, & Hoselton, 2014; McIntosh & Goodman, 2016). Similar to the process used in providing academic supports, decision rules are used to determine whether students should receive additional supports beyond Tier 2, including intensive individualized supports, such as functional analysis of behavior or behavior intervention plans, individualized mental health supports, and/or referrals to community services (Adelman & Taylor, 2012).

UNIVERSAL/TIER 1 SCREENING AND SUPPORT WITH MILITARY YOUTH

The application of MTSS with all students, including military youth, has exceptional promise, yet there is a great deal of information to be learned about the sensitivity and specificity of universal screening tools with military youth. To date, there is a limited analysis of school-based universal screening data with military youth (Gilreath et al., 2014; Lerner et al., 2009). I argue that the ESSA requirement for identifying and tracking the academic progress of military youth aligns well with the universal screening and data collection as part of MTSS, and advocate being more inclusive by including members of the National Guard and Reserves and ensuring that the concerns of families and community members are taken into account. Analyzing the responses of military families in Form 3.1 (at the end of the chapter), consulting with the military parent liaison, and holding parent forums are all ways of addressing families' concerns. Simply by having their office doors open and being visible to families, school psychologists can show that they are receptive to listening to how military families define themselves.

As introduced in Chapter 2 and expanded on more fully in Chapter 7, the ESSA now requires states to collect academic data about military students of active-duty parents through a military student identifier (Mesecar & Soifer, 2018). However, the ESSA does not define individuals in the National Guard or Reserves as members of the military unless they are in full-time active duty (Muller et al., 2016). It's important to adhere to the recommendations of the MCEC, which advocates that all dependents of all Reserve and National Guard members be included in the ESSA military data collection (Mesecar & Soifer, 2008). Nevertheless, teams engaging in MTSS supports are perfectly positioned to examine the utility of academic, behavioral, and social–emotional screeners just mentioned and the ESSA mandated data with all military youth. Further, school psychologists can take the lead in implementing comprehensive and integrated MTSS data systems that have collected much needed developmental and strengths-based information about military students (Cozza et al., 2014; Park, 2011), as recommended in Chapter 1.

Within the MTSS literature, there is a growing awareness of the effectiveness of the model with specific subpopulations that could be applied to military youth (Hernández Finch, 2012). Arguably, today's military youth are a subgroup that has not received the attention it deserves in terms of the application of universal screening and progress monitoring tools to ensure that they are successful in all aspects of school life (Cozza et al., 2014; Garcia et al., 2015). One way for schools to begin the task of addressing the needs of military youth is to disaggregate universal screening data by military status, and thereby demonstrate their intent to be inclusive of all military-connected students (Burns & Gibbons, 2012; Gilreath et al., 2014; McIntosh & Goodman, 2016).

Defining Military-Connected School-Age Youth

Defining who is within a particular subpopulation in schools is very important. There is no one universal definition as to which students and families are categorized as connected to the military, although there are both informal and formal definitions, such as students who qualify for Impact Aid (see Chapter 7) and qualify as part of ESSA reporting requirements (ESSA, 2015). Garcia et al. (2015) found that all youth connected with the military were not identified as such by their teachers and, therefore, did not benefit from services. It is critical that schools identify their military youth and track their educational progress over time within systemwide practices associated with MTSS (Gilreath et al., 2014).

Each school or district that has students connected to the military in some capacity should arrive at a definition that makes sense for their local setting and the broader community culture (Hernández Finch, 2012). Any definition that is arrived at should have significant input from the families themselves within the district that self-identify a connection within the military. For example, the American Association of School Administrators recommends that a parent liaison who is part of the local military community serve as a conduit between the school and the community. The liaison could connect with other military parents and families in the community and help school personnel arrive at a culturally sensitive definition of military youth in the district, with the ultimate goal of supporting them in being successful academically (Lerner et al., 2009). As stated earlier, children whose families are part of the National Guard and Reserves should be included as military students in the population.

Data Collection Specific to Military Youth

Presence of Military Youth and Family Military History

Form 3.1 can be completed by families when they enroll their children in a school in which any type of military involvement could be identified to school personnel. We recommend that school personnel use the form to become informed about the current and past military service of the family, including the number of deployments. In addition to questions about all forms of military service, including participation in the National Guard and Reserves, questions about other relatives, besides the parents or guardians, have been added. Families are defined very differently, and in some, extended family members, such as aunts and uncles, can have a central role and provide substantial support to the military youth and their parents. Form 3.1, or one like it, can be updated with changes in family military status and educational needs during routine and cyclical universal screening procedures. In addition, the data on a form similar to Form 3.1 can be analyzed as part of team problem-solving decisions using disaggregated data within an MTSS framework. In addition, as military families and students transition to new schools, data of this nature can be sent to a receiving school district with parental consent and/or provided to the family as part of their child's educational records and background information that they can share with a receiving school. Forms of this nature can help school districts to engage in practices consistent with the Military Interstate Children's Compact (2012).

Military-Specific Modules

Gilreath et al. (2014) created military-specific modules as a supplement to the California Healthy Kids Survey (CalSCHLS), which is administered statewide and assesses healthy student functioning, inclusive of items measuring school climate, bullying, status offenses, violent behavior, and protective factors. The modules are copyright protected and cannot be reproduced without permission. However, they can be viewed at the CalSCHLS web site at *https://calschls.org/survey-administration/downloads/#ssm_mcs*. The military modules are available in student, staff, and parent versions. Students are asked questions about the military involvement of their family members, their perceptions of stressors, military-related assets, and their views of their school's climate. Parents provide information about their military service, including their deployments and status, their rationale for school selections, their school-related service needs, and their satisfaction with their school experiences. School staff questions target whether they are aware of which students in their school building are connected to the military, whether they know what school services are available to military youth, what training they need to serve military youth, and their perceptions of how military youth feel about school climate.

PROCEDURAL CONSIDERATIONS FOR UNIVERSAL SCREENING AND SUPPORT WITH MILITARY YOUTH

From a practical standpoint, systematic demographic, parental and/or family military status, and general school-related information could be collected from military youth when they register for school to ensure that all of them are identified in the student body. Military youth who are enrolled would also participate in the universal MTSS screening procedures in the school, which often occur two or three times per year (McIntosh & Goodman, 2016). However, given the frequent family moves and school transitions of military youth, it is probable that standard screenings could be missed. Therefore, the following or similar procedures based on local preferences could be instituted:

- An MTSS team member is identified to serve as the coordinator of screening and assessment for military youth who are transitioning into the school. Ideally, the school psychologist is best suited for this role.
- Once a student is identified as a military youth, the coordinator ensures that an intake form (similar to Form 3.1) or another form is completed and reviewed. The team then reviews the information with a particular focus on the type and amount of military service and the number of deployments.
- The coordinator calls the family, welcomes them, and asks whether they have the results based on any recent universal screening data that can be sent to the school. This is also an opportunity to get a release to speak with the sending district and to coordinate any efforts related to the Military Interstate Children's Compact (2012) policies regarding registration, course enrollment, graduation requirements, and special education status.
- If the universal screening date is scheduled to occur within a month, the team may use this as a decision rule to do the screening at that time. This decision rule would be a team decision based on the local context and available resources. If the military youth just missed the screening date, then the screening needs to be completed. The team could also decide whether they would like to collect additional data with military families, such as the type of data described earlier that are included in the California military modules (Gilreath et al., 2014). A cadre of individuals on or connected with the team should be appointed to conduct the screening.
- The screening results are reviewed at the subsequent MTSS team meeting, and a decision is made as to what tier of support would be the most beneficial for the military youth.

This is one example of a universal screening process whose goal is to ensure the inclusiveness of military youth. Every school psychologist and school team will know what screening procedures are the most feasible given their local context. Inclusiveness is the key factor in helping school personnel decide how best to support military youth within an MTSS model (Kovaleski & Pederson, 2014).

PRACTICE CONSIDERATIONS FOR UNIVERSAL/TIER 1 SCREENING AND SUPPORT WITH MILITARY YOUTH

As part of the MTSS process, military youth, along with their peers in the school, should receive all universal/Tier 1 academic, behavioral, and social–emotional practices and supports. Military youth should be included in the universal screening and progress monitoring practice and in team meetings to determine which students are functioning well with Tier 1 supports and which ones need more targeted/Tier 2 and or individualized Tier 3 supports.

When delivering Tier 1 supports in a way that benefits military youth, school leaders should focus their efforts on fostering a welcoming and inclusive school climate that prioritizes caring relationships and belonging (Astor et al., 2013; De Pedro, Astor, Gilreath, Benbenishty, & Berkowitz, 2016). The efforts to create such a positive school climate will benefit all students in the school as part of universal Tier 1 supports, but are particularly necessary for military youth who change schools frequently, often finding themselves completely new to the school and community. Starting with a healthy foundation of supportive relationships for all students, and paying particular attention to honoring their resiliency and other unique talents and strengths that military youth bring to schools, will foster a healthy school climate for them (Astor et al., 2013; Park, 2011). Research on the importance of schoolwide efforts on school climate to facilitate the social development of military youth is very promising. As one example, De Pedro et al. (2016) incorporated the findings from the CalSCHLS to analyze the impact of school climate on middle and high school student self-reported peer victimization in six military-connected public-school districts. They found that school climate was a significant protective factor (though the association was weak) in student reports of peer victimization. There are a number of suggestions for developing social relationships and community spirit among military youth that are described in Chapter 4 on promoting healthy social development, particularly the activities that are part of the Purple Up Campaign to honor and recognize military youth (Military Benefits, 2019). Moreover, Chapter 5 on mental health supports discusses the importance of social relationships and a healthy school climate as part of Tier 1 supports for promoting wellness and mental health. These supports are enhancements to typical Tier 1/universal supports or could be conceptualized as more targeted interventions, depending on how they are delivered. Because they are summarized in some detail in Table 4.1 in Chapter 4 and in Chapter 5, these Tier 1 supports are not described in detail here.

PROBLEM-SOLVING CONSIDERATIONS FOR UNIVERSAL/TIER 1 SCREENING AND SUPPORT FOR MILITARY YOUTH

Problem-solving processes at the universal/Tier 1 level (focusing on the supports every student in the building is receiving), can follow structured guiding questions aligned with MTSS problem-solving models (Batsche, 2007; Brown-Chidsey & Andren, 2013; State of Florida's MTSS, 2012). Military youth receiving Tier 1 supports would automatically be part of the discussion. Tier 1 guiding questions can focus on how robust the core or schoolwide instruction is for the entire school population, regardless of whether the instruction is in the academic, behavioral, or social–emotional realm. Universal/Tier 1 systems of support are generally working if 80% or more of the school population is meeting the established school benchmark (State of Florida's MTSS, 2012). For example, when implementing the systemwide applications of SWPBS, if 80% or more of the student population generate between 0 to 1 ODRs, then these findings are generally acceptable evidence that the universal/Tier 1 behavioral support systems are being implemented at full strength or fidelity (Bohanon et al., 2006).

For military youth in a school who are receiving Tier 1 supports, a review of disaggregated universal screening data by military status is an important component of evaluating how universal/Tier 1 supports specifically affect them. However, the MTSS team will have to decide how to handle the analysis of data when the numbers of military youth are very low. For example, a rule of thumb is that when subgroups fall below 10, it is difficult to make a determination of how military youth are performing as a group. However, the MTSS team can still use these data to plan, deliver, and evaluate tiered supports with small numbers of military youth. Still, the team will need to be mindful when reporting data using low numbers of military youth, particularly in public forums. Although all students in a population, regardless of their military status, should receive universal screening and Tier 1 supports, we offer the following considerations for teams who are examining data disaggregated by military status. These considerations could lead to instruction that supplements core/Tier 1 supports for military youth through targeted interventions and/or professional development with teachers and school personnel.

Consideration 1

It would be beneficial for someone on the MTSS universal/Tier 1 team to be knowledgeable about or trained in military culture, such as a military parent liaison who may be assigned to the school or a school staff member, especially in Civilian schools (American Association of School Administrators, 2009b). Student and family voices are particularly important here, and the school could consider having a military parent on the MTSS team, if feasible, or at least ensure that a military parent is available for consultation and collaboration with the team on a periodic basis. Just as it is useful to have someone with behavioral expertise on a team that addresses system-level behavior or more individualized behavior supports (Lewis, Barrett. Sugai, & Horner, 2010), it is helpful for someone either on the team or in regular contact with it to have an understanding of military culture. This designated individual or another MTSS team member could also be responsible for tracking the changing demographics of the military population in the school over time, such as trends in the percentage of enrolled military youth and the frequency of parental deployments, and maintaining an ongoing dialogue with military families and students about what concerns they have and what they need from the school. Hall (2011), discusses the ways in which military culture is very different from Civilian life and the experiences of most educators who work with military youth. Understanding military culture involves learning the vocabulary about how the military is structured and organized, which can result in very different experiences of individual members based on their military rank (Hall, 2011). Further, understanding military culture means knowing why many individuals choose to join the military and the characteristics of military life, such as submitting to rules and prioritizing one's mission above all else (Hall, 2011). School psychologists need to understand military culture as they analyze data with military youth to help design, implement, and evaluate Tier 1/universal and other supplemental supports.

In addition to having a "go-to person" who has deep expertise about military culture, all school psychologists need to have an understanding of military culture when designing and evaluating Tier 1 supports and consulting with teachers and other school personnel about them. Luckily, well-developed modular training sessions are available for school psychologists who wish to gain more competence in understanding military culture; these sessions are described in Table 3.1.

Consideration 2

Although behavioral and social–emotional screening of all youth should be advocated (Albers & Kettler, 2014), such system-level processes may be particularly salient for military youth who face significant stressors and changes in mental health and behavioral needs across time (Chandra et al., 2011). Although military youth are viewed from a strengths-based resiliency perspective consistent with prominent military researchers (Cozza et al., 2014; Easterbrooks et al., 2013), it remains the case that they indeed face multiple sources of stress, especially the stress of deployment. If schools collect baseline social–emotional and behavioral screening data and review these data on an ongoing basis as part of benchmark procedures, then when military youth experience a stressful change (e.g., family deployments), this pool of data is available for monitoring the subsequent interventions that may be needed.

Consideration 3

MTSS teams should consider the benefits of systemwide measures of school climate and school connectedness, which are useful for the entire school population as a Tier 1 tool, would benefit military youth, and would facilitate an emphasis on wellness and an evaluation of how well the school serves as a supporting and welcoming school community (Gilreath et al., 2014). In Illinois, an ESSA indicator of school climate is captured in the statewide school data collection. The tool, the 5 Essentials Survey (Illinois State Board of Education; ISBE, 2019a), is found on the ISBE website (*www.isbe.net/Pages/5Essentials-Survey.aspx*). It is very understandable that schools may not have the resources and capacity to collect multiple screeners. We recommend, to the degree possible, that schools use already existing data that may be required for state reporting requirements or other purposes to inform MTSS team decision making.

TABLE 3.1. Online Training/Professional Development in Understanding Military Culture

Sponsor/organization	Training title	Training description	Website	Cost	Continuing education (CEUs)
Uniformed Services University of the Health Sciences Center for Deployment Psychology	Military Culture: Core Competencies for Healthcare Professionals	An eight-module online training with basic information for Civilian mental health providers about military culture and how the military is structured	*https://deploymentpsych.org/ Military-Culture-Enhancing-Competence-Course-Description*	Can be taken for free or for a $15 CEU fee	2 CEU hours for psychologists/ counselors
VHA Training; U.S. Department of Veterans Affairs	Military Culture: Core Competencies for Healthcare Professionals; Self-Assessment and Introduction to Military Ethos	A four-module online training focused on the experiences of post-9/11 service members and the deployment cycle; covers stigma in seeking mental health treatment	*www.train.org/vha/ course/1056248/*	Can be taken free with registration and completion of a survey	2 CEU hours for psychologists

SPECIAL CONSIDERATIONS FOR SECONDARY/TIER 2 SYSTEMS OF SUPPORT WITH MILITARY YOUTH

Once a solid foundation of universal screening procedures and supports for all students, including military youth, at the universal/Tier 1 level has been achieved, schools can begin the task of determining which supplemental supports can be delivered at the secondary/Tier 2 level and with which students, including subpopulations of military youth (Brown-Chidsey & Andren, 2013; Burns & Gibbons, 2012). Military youth may be accommodated within standard protocol approaches or other secondary/Tier 2 supports that are often already available in schools, and they may benefit from these supports as much as their non-military peers (VanDerHeyden, n.d.). However, owing to the specialized needs that some military youth have, it may be the case that they would do better with secondary/Tier 2 interventions targeted specifically for them. Problem-solving teams in each school or district are in the best position to make these decisions if the data so indicate. Military parents may also need ongoing support. This assistance could be provided by supplemental groups intended specifically for military families and offered in a school setting, such as Families Over Coming Under Stress (FOCUS) school-based groups that target family resiliency (Garcia et al., 2015) or by community partnerships, such as the After Deployment Adaptive Parenting Tools (ADAPT) program (Gewirtz et al., 2009) which focuses on parenting skills and family adjustment following a deployment. Table 3.2 provides a brief summary of each of these well-researched and widely implemented targeted programs for military families for school psychologists to consider. Determining whether programs are offered to family members in person or online would need to be based on a family's accessibility to the place where the programs are delivered and whether all family members are in one location to participate in the program.

In addition, at the secondary/Tier 2 level, some supplemental, targeted efforts to improve school climate for all students can be offered, with particular attention given to military-connected youth who may not have established community roots and connections. As a simple example, at least one adult in the school can connect with and serve as a mentor for each military youth. The adult mentor could support and encourage military youth to join clubs, sport teams, or other social groups as ways of facilitating school connectedness and a positive school climate (Arnold, Garner, Neale-McFall, & Nunnery, 2011; Centers for Disease Control and Prevention, 2009). The Military Child Education Coalition (2019a) Student 2 Student program, described in more detail in Chapter 4 (Table 4.2), offers another excellent way for peers to engage with peers as military youth transition to a new school setting.

If the results of behavioral and social–emotional screening, as well as follow-up assessments, support the need for mental health interventions that address trauma, grief, complicated grief, anxiety, or depressive symptomatology, then the school could provide group supports in these arenas, including specialized modifications for military youth (Cohen, Mannarino, & Deblinger, 2010). Tiers 2 and 3 mental health supports are described in more detail and summarized in Chapter 5, Table 5.1.

TABLE 3.2. Comparison of ADAPT and FOCUS Targeted Parenting Programs

Summary of major content	Delivery method	Military population of focus	Relevant websites
ADAPT (Gewirtz et al., 2009) Focuses on parenting skills and readjusting to family life after a deployment	In person at military installations Telehealth/online Online video curriculum	Originally developed for parents in the National Guard/Reserves and now expanding to Special Operations forces and active-duty army families	Main website: *https://itr.umn.edu/adapt/how-to-participate* To sign up for newsletter and see parenting toolkits organized by age: *https://itr.umn.edu/adapt/resources-for-military-parents*
FOCUS (Garcia et al., 2015) There are several variations of the program, with the focus being on building family resilience in the following areas: emotional regulation, problem solving, goal setting, managing trauma, and stress reminders	In person at military installations Mobile app with family resources: *https://focusproject.org/mobile-app* Also offers consultation to community service providers and families, as well as educational workshops Online educational tool with videos: *https://focusproject.org/focus-world*	Developed for active-duty military families	Main website: *https://focusproject.org* Map of locations: *https://focusproject.org/contact* Online accessible newsletter with family activities: *https://focusproject.org/focus-quarterly*

SPECIAL CONSIDERATIONS FOR TERTIARY/TIER 3 SYSTEMS OF SUPPORT WITH MILITARY YOUTH

Finally, along a continuum of support, military youth may require intensive and individualized supports, despite the effort to deliver the most solid universal/Tier 1 and supplemental/Tier 2 supports possible. Military youth may receive these supports either in the school or through collaboration and in careful coordination with community-based professionals (Adelman & Taylor, 2012). Families and youth with intensive needs may also benefit from careful wraparound planning, which is a strengths-based approach in which the needs are determined by the family members and the people on the team are not necessarily professionals, but are included for their ability to serve as natural supports for the family (Bruns et al., 2004). Wraparound planning is consistent with the strengths-based and resiliency perspective taken in this book. Military liaisons or other individuals who naturally provide support to the family during military-related family experiences, such as deployments and transitions, could fit well into a wraparound planning process. The following case example illustrates how a school district may apply the full range of MTSS procedures in the service of military youth within a school district.

CASE EXAMPLE OF A UNIVERSAL SCREENING/MTSS APPROACH IN A CIVILIAN MIDDLE SCHOOL

Allen Middle School is located in a suburb just outside a midsize city in the northeast. It is part of a consolidated Civilian school district that has a military base within the district boundaries and educates children in grades 6–8. The school district is considered a high-achieving one that feeds into a large and highly academically ranked high school within the state. There is some racial and ethnic diversity, with approximately 25% of the students of Latinx background, 20% Asian/Pacific Islander, 20% African American, and 35% White. Two elementary schools feed into the middle school. Meadowood Elementary serves the majority of elementary-age military youth within the district (100 of the 300 typical enrollment, on the average), while the second elementary school, Landmark Elementary, has no military children (0 of the 200 students), given the geographic boundaries of the military base within the district's city limits. Therefore, students entering Allen Middle School have very different elementary school experiences, in that non-military youth may or may not have interacted with peers connected with the military. Meadowood Elementary has engaged in significant work in honoring and serving military youth, such as having ongoing celebrations and support for military families, peer mentoring programs, family support groups, parenting classes, and coordination with after-school child care within the community. Allen Middle School has about 20%–25% military student enrollment, but it varies because students move in and out owing to military transitions on the base.

Allen Middle School administered a fall survey of school climate, which included items related to feelings of acceptance and bullying. Primary concerns raised as a result of this survey is that relatively fewer military youth compared to their non-military peers feel connected to the school and affirm that they would have an adult to go to if they had an issue or problem (approximately 67%), relative to the about 80% of the overall student population reporting positive school connectedness and having at least one identified adult within the school to turn to. Overall, about 20% of the school population believes that bullying is occurring, and there were no appreciable differences in the responses of military versus non-military youth, by racial or ethnic group, or English language learner status. All three schools have been implementing SWPBS for several years (Bohanon et al., 2006). Landmark and Meadowood elementary schools and Allen Middle School have collaborated to develop common behavioral expectations and a common language to support teaching and acknowledging behavior. Given these data, the school universal team decides to do the following:

- To address the systemwide social issues of bullying and school connectedness, lessons from the *Bullying and Harassment Prevention in Positive Behavior Support: Expect Respect* handbook (Stiller, Nese, Tomlanovich, Horner, & Ross, 2013) are put in place as classwide enhancements that supplement the universal SWBPS supports. The handbook contains lesson plans that are aligned with SWPBS and can be delivered in a series of push-in classroom lessons. These lessons are implemented by teachers at the middle school during advisory periods with the help of the school psychologist and other school-based mental health professionals on the MTSS team. Not only is the program aligned with the already ongoing SWPBS supports, it is also targeted for middle and high school students on issues specific to bullying, which appears to be more of a systemwide problem despite the use of SWPBS. In preparation for the delivery of lessons, the school staff receives training, coaching, and modeling of the delivery from the school psychologist. On a systemwide level, bullying policies and practices are reviewed with the students, families, and staff at the beginning of the school year and then on a quarterly basis. A booster SWPBS universal teaching session that entails practicing the schoolwide expectations is also delivered schoolwide three times a year to supplement the universal SWPBS supports.

- A Tier 2/supplemental group with military youth is initiated, which involves weekly meetings with the school psychologist or school social worker and the enactment of a mentoring program with school staff and students. A parent liaison, who is connected with the military, assists and consults with this process. The parent liaison also helps to establish support groups with families in the community.

- A Student-2-Student program (Military Child Education Coalition, 2019a) is initiated on a volunteer basis for students in the military to be paired with non-military students to foster understanding and connections with one another.

- For cases in which more intensive social–emotional supports are needed, the school psychologist and school social worker provide mental health support, consult with community service providers familiar with military life, and also help to invoke wraparound services (Bruns et al., 2004) by collaborating with community mental health service providers (Adelman & Taylor, 2012).

- The entire school professional staff, including the teachers in the elementary and middle schools, receive training and professional development in military culture. A military family liaison is assigned to the school district, with more of their time devoted to Allen Middle Schools, consult with the staff to improve relationships among teachers and military students due to the high number of military youth who do not feel a sense of connectedness to an adult in the building.

- The district initiates a day of service at the start of the school year for both elementary schools and the middle school, in which military families and students are honored for serving their country. Each month, a military family is acknowledged for their service. These activities lead up to the Month of the Military Child in April, in which the Purple Up Campaign is conducted in all schools in the district (Military Benefits, 2019).

- To evaluate the progress, particularly in the areas of bullying and harassment, ODRs are reviewed monthly. Universal social–emotional and behavioral screening data are reviewed by the MTSS during the three benchmark periods as part of universal screening procedures. The evaluation of efforts across the tiers of support for the overall student population and for military youth are the focus of the data analysis and problem-solving meetings.

This case scenario is one example of an approach that a school district can take to begin providing much-deserved services to all students, including military youth. Universal screening and an MTSS framework (State of Florida's MTSS, 2012) can be useful when aligned with public health models recommended by military researchers (Gilreath et al., 2014). School psychologists, who are knowledgeable about and trained in MTSS, can be integral to leading an MTSS team effort and applying their expertise as they carefully consider and support the educational needs of military youth. Our military youth have been greatly underserved in our schools, with very little attention given to the importance of system-level data collection in systematically documenting their many strengths and developmental needs and providing educational supports, when necessary, earlier along an MTSS continuum (Cozza et al., 2014; Garcia et al., 2015; Gilreath et al., 2014).

FORM 3.1

Family Military Service and Brief Educational History

Name of Student:

Entering Grade:

Address:

Phone:

E-mail:

Family Military Service

Parent/Guardian #1 Name:

1. Are you a **veteran** of the military?   Yes ____   No ____
2. Are you **active duty** in the military?   Yes ____   No ____
3. Are you a member of the **National Guard/Reserves**?   Yes ____   No ____

If you answered "yes" to questions 1, 2, or 3, please complete the following:

    Branch of Military _____

    Years of Service _____

    Number of Deployments _____

Total Months/Years of Deployment, Dates and Locations

    a. Deployment #1 _____

    b. Deployment #2 _____

    c. Deployment #3 _____

    d. Deployment #4 _____

Parent/Guardian #2 Name:

1. Are you a **veteran** of the military?   Yes ____   No ____
2. Are you **active duty** in the military?   Yes ____   No ____
3. Are you a member of the **National Guard/Reserves**?   Yes ____   No ____

If you answered "yes" to questions 1, 2, or 3, please complete the following:

    Branch of Military _____

    Years of Service _____

    Number of Deployments _____

(continued)

From *School Supports for Students in Military Families* by Pamela Fenning. Copyright © 2021 The Guilford Press. Permission to photocopy this form is granted to purchasers of this book for personal use or use with students (see copyright page for details). Purchasers can download additional copies of this form (see the box at the end of the table of contents).

Family Military Service and Brief Educational History *(page 2 of 3)*

Total Months/Years of Deployment and Location

    a. Deployment #1 _____

    b. Deployment #2 _____

    c. Deployment #3 _____

    d. Deployment #4 _____

Other Family Member Military Service

Please list any other close family members or those you consider part of your family who are engaged in military service and provide family relationship (e.g., older sibling, uncle, grandparent).

_____

_____

Please describe the type of military service and dates, including active-duty status and deployments.

_____

_____

If you are enrolling more than one student, you only need to answer the questions about parent or guardian and other family military service once.

Educational History of Student

Please complete the following for each student you are enrolling:

Please list the previous schools attended (include city and state), with dates attended.

Please list any prior educational services, including speech and language, counseling, or any special education services.

(continued)

Family Military Service and Brief Educational History *(page 3 of 3)*

If your child has a current individualized education plan (IEP), please contact _____,
Director of Special Education, who can ensure that a team reviews the previous educational services and works with a team to ensure continuity of services

Please describe any educational needs or ways that the school can assist you and your family as you transition to our community and school.

Is there something that you would like for us to know about your child that we should have asked, but didn't?

Please let us know how we can assist you and your family. For families with military service, we will provide some information on services that the school offers in working with military families as well as some military resources and information that may be useful. Feel free to contact _____ **should you have any questions.**
_____ **is the parent liaison at**
_____ **and is also a resource who can assist you.**

CHAPTER 4

Promoting Healthy Social Development

IMPACT OF MILITARY TRANSITIONS ON SOCIAL DEVELOPMENT AND RELATIONSHIPS

Chapter 2 examined in depth how the different educational institutions that military youth attend (e.g., Civilian schools, DoD-administered schools, and international schools) affect their lives as students. This chapter focuses on ways to help military students and their families make healthy social connections and build relationships within the school building and the broader community. Military youth have a high probability of experiencing multiple school transitions and family relocations compared with non-military peers who are more likely to live and grow up in the same community with the same peers. As a result, entering new social situations and making friends can be a potential challenge for military students. The same holds true for parents and other family members who may feel isolated and disconnected throughout many deployments, underscoring the importance of considering the entire family unit when helping to facilitate social supports. Parents may find the transition to a neighborhood as equally isolating as their children, because they may not have any previously established social relationships in the community. They may not know the social culture of the geographic region or school, and not be privy to the unwritten social norms that guide how families meet and socialize with one another. Moreover, the typical ways that parents become socially engaged and meet one another, such as through volunteering opportunities, may not be feasible for military families who have other commitments during the day and/or might not have received school communications about them. Military families may not know about school functions and community events, depending on when they moved into a community, and the ways in which they are publicized. For example, military families may miss school volunteering opportunities that are publicized at the beginning of the school year. In some communities where there is a high military presence or a base school exclusively for military children, the opportunity to make connections with those who have a similar lifestyle and who understand the challenges that military families face is woven in to the fabric of the community. However, more times than not, military children attend neighborhood Civilian schools (Clever & Segal, 2013) with non-military peers who have different experiences and where opportunities for military families to socially engage with the school community may not even be considered. Military youth and their families may require the specialized attention of school personnel so they receive the necessary social support to ensure that they are welcomed to the school and have opportunities for positive social interactions.

SOCIAL SUPPORTS WITH MILITARY YOUTH AND FAMILIES: ONE SIZE DOES NOT FIT ALL

When considering the type and intensity of social supports with military youth, it should be emphasized that there is no single approach to fostering healthy social development that works for everyone. In addition to the type of school setting, one factor that influences social opportunities for military youth and their families is the parents' military branch of service. For example, children whose parents serve in the National Guard and Reserves (Milburn & Lightfoot, 2013) are less likely than those in other military branches to live on or near military bases (Lemmon & Chartrand, 2009, as cited in Milburn & Lightfoot, 2013). In discussing this group of children, Kudler and Porter (2013) state, "They usually live far from military bases and military treatment facilities, and they may be strangers to the institutions of military life" (p. 168). As previously discussed, school psychologists can use data collection tools to help their colleagues better understand the varied backgrounds of military youth and families, such as the Family Military Service and Brief Educational History form (Form 3.1 in Chapter 3), or a similar one. Knowing the school and family context, not a one-size-fits-all mindset, is what truly matters in supporting the social development of military youth. Aside from the frequent moves and transitions that characterize the social lives of military children (Bradshaw et al., 2010), all military youth navigate specific social developmental milestones. As such, I offer a brief general overview of social development described by prominent developmental theorists, such as Erik Erikson (1963). The rest of the chapter is devoted to a discussion of three major developmental and instructional levels: (1) infancy and early childhood, (2) the elementary school years, and (3) adolescence in middle and high school. We highlight special considerations and recommendations that support military youth at each of these developmental stages (Sumner, Boisvert, & Andersen, 2016).

APPLICATIONS OF SOCIAL DEVELOPMENTAL THEORY WITH MILITARY YOUTH

School psychologists and other readers of this book will likely have an educational background in child development. Nevertheless, we briefly review the pivotal theoretical work of Erik Erikson's (1963) eight stage theory of psychosocial development since his theory has greatly influenced my own views of social development.

Social Development in Infancy and Early Childhood

Stage 1: Infancy

Stage 1, infancy, is described as "Trust" versus "Mistrust" and involves an understanding that the primary caretaker can leave, but comes back (Baker-Smith & Moore, 2001; Erikson, 1963). Children also learn to "trust" themselves and their basic instincts. School-based mental health professionals, particularly those working in early childhood settings, can provide resources and support for families of young children in preparation for, during, and after deployments. For example, Sesame Street offers excellent tips and resources for the youngest military family members, such as continuing predicable routines like nighttime rituals (Sesame Workshop, 2019). Another idea provided by Sesame Street is the creation of a comforting object, like a stuffed pillow using the military service member's shirts, which the child can turn to as a reminder of the parent. It is particularly important in modern times to support families with children of all ages, because of the length, frequency, and unpredictability of deployments in recent years (Stepka & Callahan, 2016).

Stage 2: Autonomy

The second stage, "Autonomy" versus "Shame and Doubt," occurs during the toddler years (ages 1.5–3.5 years) (Baker-Smith & Moore, 2001). The child begins to explore the world and to test things in the environment in a purposeful way. If this stage isn't mastered, then the child experiences shame in the form of feeling exposed to the world, rather than having a sense of individual control and feeling good about oneself (Erikson, 1963). In their writing about military-involved families with young children, Stepka and Callahan (2016) stress the role of attachment theory (Bowlby, 1969) when thinking about how to support the social development of infants and toddlers, and in understanding how early parent and/or caregiver and child interactions are necessary for a secure attachment (Bowlby, 1969). Finding ways to foster parent–child interactions affects future social relationships that are formed with peers and other adults in later years.

Stage 3: Initiative versus Guilt

In Erikson's third stage, "Initiative" versus "Guilt" (ages 3.5–5.5 years) (Baker-Smith & Moore, 2001), the child begins to engage in goal-directed behavior by using motor and mental abilities acquired in earlier stages. If tasks are not mastered at this stage, then the child develops guilt feelings.

Considerations and Recommendations for Supporting the Social Development of Infants and Young Children in Military Families

Given that the social development of infants and young children (ages 3–5) in military families is an underexplored topic of study, Osofsky and Molinda Chartrand (2013) underscore the importance of understanding attachment theory (Bowlby, 1969) when considering how to best support them, because attachment figures may not be present when a family service member is deployed. Osofsky and Molinda Chartrand (2013) stress that one cannot assume that deployments and other separations do not affect young children since even children at this age are capable of understanding changes in routines and of feeling the impact of being separated from loved ones (Osofsky & Molinda Chartrand, 2013). Stepka and Callahan (2016) also emphasize the importance of attachment theory in understanding the social worlds of infants and toddlers in military families. The attachment concept "theory of the mind," in which toddlers begin to differentiate their emotions and feelings from those of others, is an important attachment concept for early childhood educators to reference in their work with young military families (Stepka & Callahan, 2016) and for school psychologists to highlight when consulting with teachers and families.

With a grounding in infant and/or early childhood developmental theories, such as attachment theory (Bowlby,1969) and psychosocial development (Erikson, 1963), school psychologists can support the social development of infants and young children connected with the military by doing the following: (1) support parent or caregiver and child attachment, (2) facilitate high-quality preschool and infant and early childhood developmental experiences, and (3) be particularly mindful about young military family and childhood stressors and experiences in deployment situations.

Support of the Parent or Caregiver and Child Attachment. The efforts of school psychologists who work with military youth need to be considered in a military context that may involve long absences of one or both parents, changes in caregivers, and frequent relocations and deployments. Table 3.2 in Chapter 3 provides links for accessible family resources for military families who have children of all ages, including infants and toddlers (Garcia et al., 2015; Gewirtz et al., 2009). Table 4.1 features two additional useful resources to promote secure parent–infant attachment and the healthy social development of our youngest children in military families.

Facilitating High-Quality Preschool and Early Childhood Experiences. The structure and routines of preschool, which afford opportunities to interact with other families with young children could serve as a protective factor for military families. The Military One Source resource in Table 4.1 provides important information about preschool options for military families, including Head Start and Sure Start Preschool, which are described

TABLE 4.1. Resources to Promote Positive Early Parenting Interactions

Name of resource	Brief description	Website
Military One Source (n.d.).	This website contains information for support available specifically for service members, such as the New Parent Support Program (e.g., prenatal classes, nurse visits) and the Family Readiness System (e.g., supports related to moving, deployment, emergency situations, child maltreatment, and healthy parent–child interactions).	*www.militaryonesource.mil/family-relationships/parenting-and-children/parenting-and-children-resources*
Sesame Street for Military Families (Sesame Workshop, 2019)	The beloved *Sesame Street* characters tackle a variety of military family issues with videos and downloadable .pdf resources. The topics range widely from celebrating birthdays remotely, deployment, family routines (e.g., bedtime stories), and processing grief, which can be engaged in through video and/or online. The website is organized and searchable by topic.	*https://sesamestreetformilitaryfamilies.org*

on the Military One website (Military One Source, n. d). School psychologists and other early childhood professionals can be integral to helping young families access high-quality, parent–baby interaction groups, community playgroups, and early childhood and/or preschool educational experiences that are the best fit for their family. Through these early childhood and community supports, these professionals can provide psychoeducation around a variety of parenting issues that may arise with young military families, and extend support for parents preparing for deployment or returning from one.

School-based mental health professionals can also access military families with young children through required federal child find procedures. Through Child Find, Wrightslaw notes, "schools are required to locate, identify and evaluate all children with disabilities from birth to 21" (Wright & Wright, 2018). Under Early Intervention Regulations (34, C.F.R. 303.321), by their third birthday, children with disabilities must be identified for special education. Furthermore, states are encouraged to provide interventions with infants and toddlers as early as possible and to promote coordination among agencies that serve young children (Wright & Wright, 2018). In particular, military families with young children living in Civilian settings and serving in the National Guard or Reserves may not have the robust supports and accessible services available to military families living in military installations. (Chapter 2 discussed these varied school settings in depth, and Chapter 7 discusses the legal aspects of being a military youth in a DoD, overseas, or Civilian environment.) Identification and outreach with families in Civilian settings could occur through posting notices for early childhood screenings in community preschools, religious institutions, recreation centers, local park districts, military installations, National Guard or

Reserve buildings, grocery stores, or playgrounds and libraries where families with young children are likely to go. For military families whose children live in the catchment area of a DoD school, school liaison officers are important collaborators to communicate with about what social supports exist for young families in their area (DoDEA, 2019b). Even if young children do not qualify for early intervention services, school psychologists can still share information and connect families with local and military-related resources should the need arise.

Unique Considerations during Deployment. School psychologists need to have an understanding of the unique aspects of deployment with young military families. They should consult and provide psychoeducation with early childhood educators, community child care centers, other families, and organizations that support young children. Trautmann, Alhusen, and Gross (2015) conducted a systematic literature review of young children (birth to 5) of deployed military parents. The authors specifically examined 26 studies focused on behavioral and mental health issues of parents and young children in military families. The reader is referred to Trautmann et al. (2015) for an analysis of each of the studies they reviewed, since the focus here is mainly on the findings related to children's social development. The key findings were that more deployments and those of longer duration were associated with higher parental reported stress and depressive symptoms (Barker & Berry, 2009, as reported in Trautmann et al., 2015). Military spouses raising young children on their own during military deployments were particularly likely to report mental health concerns (Barker & Berry, 2009, as cited in Trautmann et al., 2015). Deployed parents also reported distress related to parenting (Trautmann et al., 2015). During reintegration following deployment, military fathers had parenting concerns about asking for advice, reconnecting with their children, positively communicating with their spouses and children, and disciplining their children (Trautmann et al., 2015). Fathers who returned home with injuries or posttraumatic stress disorder (PTSD) perceived their reintegration as particularly challenging (Trautmann et al., 2015). Behavioral concerns were highest among toddlers (3–5-year-olds) of deployed parents compared to children younger than 3 (Flake et al., 2009, as cited in Trautmann et al., 2015), whereas children younger than 3 years old had more attachment-related concerns, especially during reintegration following a deployment (Barker & Berry, 2009, as cited in Trautmann et al., 2015). These findings might be expected given the social developmental theories described earlier. They also underscore the importance of sharing the family and parenting resources found in Table 4.1 and in Table 3.2 in Chapter 3 related to parenting skills, parental stress, and resiliency.

Social Development during the Elementary School Years

Stage 4: Industry versus Inferiority

Stage 4, "Industry" versus "Inferiority," (ages 5.5–12 years) is described by Erikson (1963) as the "school years" or latency period, in which children master the tasks that are deemed important within their particular culture. This is the stage of productivity and industriousness. A child who does not adequately master the stage four tasks has feelings of inferiority. In this stage, Erikson describes the dangers experienced by individuals and society when children recognize that discriminatory factors in schools (e.g., race or ethnicity, parental income) predict their value and place in the working order of society rather than their effort and desire to achieve (Erikson, 1963). In stage four, children are taught the skills that are valuable in their specific culture, whether it be one of labor in an industrial society, farming in an agrarian environment, or academic achievement in a more postindustrial context (Erikson, 1963).

During this "middle childhood period," there are many academic and social demands (Jones, Barnes, Bailey, & Doolittle, 2017). Although researchers and educators have slightly different definitions for the age range of middle childhood, there is common agreement that significant social developmental growth takes place (Eccles, 1999). According to Eccles (who defined middle childhood as between 6 and 10 years of age), children of this developmental period are focused on being accepted by their peers and frequently engage in social comparison with one another. In elementary schools, social networks are expanded beyond families to other adults who supervise them for many hours (e.g., teachers or coaches), and children begin spending significant portions of their day with peers. It is, therefore, not surprising that schools across the world begin formal instruction, however defined, around age 6 (Eccles, 1999).

Supporting the Social Development of Elementary-Age Children in Military Families

School psychologists need to be sensitive to the values and beliefs of all families, including military personnel who identify strongly with the military cultural values described in Chapter 3. At this developmental stage, peers start to become very important in the lives of young children. Elementary-age youth connected with the military have to negotiate these important social developmental tasks, while often navigating the frequent moves and transitions that go along with military life. School psychologists and other school professionals can help to support military youth as they navigate new social circumstances to ensure they are not only included by the school community, but also honored by peers and adults. Specifically, school psychologists can do the following: (1) help to ensure that school environments and classrooms are warm and welcoming when elementary school military youth transition, and (2) facilitate the ongoing recognition of military youth through both formally and less formally structured activities and efforts.

Creating Warm, Welcoming Schools and Classrooms with Military Youth. It is important that all military youth, including school-age children, be welcomed to new schools and socially supported and mentored by peers and teachers throughout the year. This can be done through formal programs and informal means. An example of a formal program is an initiative that has been implemented with active chapters across the United States and around the world is Student 2 Student, an initiative of the MCEC (Military Child Education Coalition, 2019a). Student 2 Student is an effort that matches Civilian students with military students who transition to new schools to make them feel welcome and to pair them with a "buddy" to make the experience a positive one. There are variations of the program for each developmental level, organized by elementary, middle, and high school levels. Additional information about the online Student 2 Student initiative is presented in Table 4.2 (pp. 58–59).

Another program, Stay Strong with Schools, a school-based intervention, was evaluated by Ohye, Jakubovic, Zakarian, and Bui (2020) using a randomized control trial method to evaluate the impact with 56 elementary military-connected youth across a school year. The three main components provided to the children receiving the intervention were: (1) a 1-hour professional development session with school professionals that focused on the Stay Strong with Schools coordinated outreach with military youth and psychoeducation around the deployment cycle, (2) an outreach effort led by a guidance counselor early in the year to families of military youth that included a resiliency plan, and (3) classroom-based activities and a schoolwide event to increase awareness of the experiences of military families and the contributions that they make. The reader is referred to the study for the complete findings about internalizing and externalizing behaviors. Military youth who received the intervention rated their social support as statistically increasing across the intervention year based on The Child and Adolescent Social Support Scale (Malecki, Demaray, & Elliott, 2000). In contrast, military youth in the control group showed statistically significant reductions in their perceived social support during the year. These positive findings document the utility of a relatively low cost and low-resource intervention that shows exceptional promise for facilitating social supports among military youth. School psychologists can build upon this work by replicating this study and evaluating its impact on the social development of military youth across the country.

In elementary school, classroom teachers are particularly critical to the social development of military students since children at this level typically spend a great deal of time in one classroom managed by a primary teacher. Therefore, classroom teachers are the linchpins in cultivating a warm and inviting classroom for military youth who make frequent transitions, because these teachers are the primary adult anchors in middle childhood. Coaches and other adults who supervise extracurricular activities also play a role. Morgan and Ross (2013) suggest a number of recommendations for teachers and administrators to enhance the social development of elementary-age military youth, including simply knowing which students in their school are connected to the military, offering themselves and school counselors as speakers regarding any concerns, offering student shadowing programs for new military students, and running after-school groups, especially during deployments and other times of stress.

Teachers and other professionals, such as school psychologists and social workers, should be particularly mindful of activities and routines during the day that involve peers, particularly for transitioning military youth. For instance, assignments for class projects and collaborative work require particular attention on the part of teachers and consultative efforts from school psychologists to ensure that military youth feel comfortable and connected socially to peers as well as to adults within the school. Ensuring that incoming military students have a peer to sit with at lunch, for example, is a small gesture that can go a long way.

To facilitate accessible professional development for all school personnel who want to create a welcoming and warm environment in which to nurture military youth, the MCEC has created a number of Ted Talks that specifically deal with training professionals about how to support military children (Military Child Education Coalition, 2019c). One of the lessons features information about school transitions and the critical role of the first weeks of school (Table 4.2 provides the link to access the Ted Talk). Professional development accessed through these easy-to-locate and already developed resources can help to foster the social development of military youth and provide support at key times.

Facilitating Ongoing Recognition of Military Youth on an Ongoing Basis through Formally Structured Programs and Less Formally Structured Activities and Efforts. School psychologists can lead efforts to recognize the contributions of military youth and their families, in which the entire school can participate. These efforts will help create a community of acceptance and foster the social development and acceptance of military youth. One formal program and set of activities implemented across the country is The Purple Up Campaign (DoDEA, 2019a), which consists of a series of events that pay tribute to the unique contributions that military youth and families make to society. Commonly associated with activities such as saluting military families at school events, hosting assemblies, and wearing purple to celebrate the blended colors of all military branches, these events can be integrated into the school curriculum year-round. "Purple Up for Military Kids" celebrations can be offered in any of the schools that military youth attend, including those at DoDEA installations and Civilian public schools, as well as at local businesses (Military Benefits, 2019). April is designated as the Month of the Military Child, and the months leading up to it could culminate in a special assembly for military children. The DoDEA website has additional resources specific to the Month of the Military Child. It goes without saying that military youth should have a voice in deciding when and how these celebrations take place. These activities could be a wonderful opportunity for elementary-age children to learn about their military peers and gain a respect and understanding for the valuable contributions they and their families make. Table 4.2 provides more information about the Purple Up campaign and a link to its website.

In addition to accessing and implementing formally developed programs and activities, school personnel and administrators can engage in relatively simple actions that pay tribute to military youth and make them part of the social fabric of communities and educational settings. For example, in a school that I am familiar with, the principal asked military service parents to raise the U.S. flag on a daily basis. This and other brief activities and spontaneous conversations can create an atmosphere that celebrates military families not through "one-time/one-shot" approaches, but through mindful and daily considerations of the enormous sacrifices that they make to support youths' healthy social development and their ability to thrive.

Social Development during Adolescence

Stage 5: Identity versus Isolation and Stage 6: Young Adulthood

The next two stages are experienced during adolescence and young adulthood, respectively: Stage 5, "Identity" versus "Role Confusion" and Stage 6, "Intimacy" versus "Isolation" (Baker-Smith & Moore, 2001). Stage five represents a transition from "childhood" to "adolescence," in which the major tasks involve taking on social roles and establishing ego identity (Erikson, 1963). Stage five coincides with the advent of puberty and rapid body growth at the level experienced during early childhood (Erikson, 1963). Sexual maturity occurs during Stage 5. Youth become very concerned with what others think and form social groups based on cliques that determine who is in the "in crowd" and the "out crowd" (Erikson, 1963). Youth identity is exemplified by overidentification with peers at this stage (Erikson, 1963). In stage 6, young adulthood, the major task is that of "intimacy versus isolation," or that of establishing intimate partnerships versus experiencing isolation.

Stage 7: Generativity versus Stagnation and Stage 8: Integrity versus Despair

The final two stages of "Generativity" versus "Stagnation" (Stage 7) and "Integrity" versus "Despair" (Stage 8) occur during adulthood. These stages involve the adult tasks of producing and guiding the next generation (Stage 7), and integrating one's ego identity, acquiring maturity, and accepting the finite aspects of one's life (Stage 8) (Erikson, 1963).

Supporting the Social Development of Adolescents in Military Families

Adolescents with families in the military may encounter new social situations and social groupings with peers and adults they do not know and whose social patterns may already be quite entrenched. Therefore, adolescence may be a particularly sensitive period for military youth who may need particular supports to successfully navigate social environments for their healthy social development. Supports such as Student 2 Student (MCEC, 2019), described in Table 4.2, can help military-connected adolescents with these social transitions.

As military youth graduate to middle and high school, critical social developmental issues emerge, as entry into adolescence is marked by the formation of cliques and close identification with one's peer group, according to Erikson (1963). As described earlier, military youth are subjected to frequent relocations and school transitions, on average, a total of nine school transitions during their K–12 years (Kitmitto et al., 2011, as cited in Astor et al., 2013). For adolescents, these school transitions coincide with a developmental period in which peer relationships play a key role.

To further understand the stressors experienced by military-connected students and how schools could ease the pressure on them, Bradshaw et al. (2010) conducted focus groups with military adolescents, their parents, and school personnel (e.g., teachers, counselors, and school psychologists). The participants were drawn from eight military bases representing all military branches, and the student participants attended Civilian public schools serving the bases. The participating students ranged in age from 12–18, with a median age of 14.6 years, and an average of over five military-related moves. Using a phenomenological approach to the research, the authors applied a family stress framework to the data coding and analysis. A number of the Bradshaw et al. (2010) study findings are relevant to an improved understanding of social development among military adolescents and how school psychologists can assist them. The findings revealed a number of reported stressors around social relationships with peers and making friends. For example, students commented on the difficulties in making and keeping close friends when transitioning to new schools. With respect to the friendships made among military youth, separation from long-time friends and observable changes in relationships and behaviors leading up to family moves were also noted. Another key factor expressed by the participants was the timing of the move, particularly among adolescents breaking into established cliques that are common in this age group. Another additional pressure tied to school transitions is the timing of extracurricular activities that foster social identity and peer relationships. Students may transition to a new school after tryouts are over for the year, making it difficult to join a particular sport. It may become difficult to become involved in student government, in which those who are better known may be more likely to be selected compared with newly-enrolling military students. At the same time, the participants noted several advantages of military life. For example, school staff described military youth as adaptable and more mature than their civilian peers. Military youth also noted several personal strengths specific to the military, such as being able to handle transitions and blend more easily into new social situations. Some military youth noted that they enjoyed the opportunity to travel abroad as part of the moves they made with their families. Parents, school staff, and the students themselves mentioned that military youth have a greater acceptance and appreciation of diversity. Finally, it should be noted that military youth reported that the strongest school connections were with other peers compared to adult staff.

Based on these data collected with military youth (Bradshaw et al., 2010) and our knowledge of the developmental importance of peers in adolescence, we suggest the following specific ways in which school psychologists can support their social development: (1) facilitate opportunities for military youth to participate in extracurricular activities, such as clubs and sports teams; (2) ensure that student voices related to social priorities and adjustment are captured, particularly those of adolescents who are transitioning into a new school environment; and (3) facilitate universal social–emotional and behavioral screening as described in Chapter 3, including considering and/or adapting the process outlined in Chapter 3 for capturing data with military adolescents who are not enrolled in school when periodic benchmark data are collected.

Facilitating Participation in Extracurricular Activities. Extracurricular activities, such as sports teams, clubs, and other student-led groups can be a tremendous opportunity for military adolescents to make friends, build social competencies through teamwork, and gain leadership experiences. For those military adolescents who transition into schools at a point in the year in which they miss tryouts for competitive sports teams, school psychologists should do all they can to create opportunities to get them involved. They should also ensure that the entire school community is aware of the agreements within the Military Interstate Compact (Interstate Commission on Educational Opportunity for Military Children Rules, 2012). The agreement calls for the facilitation of military students' participation in extracurricular activities, but does not guarantee a spot on a school team, for example (Fenning et al., 2013). Military youth could be encouraged to start a club with and for military youth in the school if one does not exist.

Ensuring that Student Voices Are Captured. School psychologists and other school personnel, using a strengths-based and resiliency approach (Easterbrooks et al., 2013; Lerner et al., 2009; Masten, 2013b), should listen to the opinions of military youth and their families most affected by decisions that are made. While ensuring that the voices of youth are heard is advisable at all developmental stages, the voices of military adolescents are particularly important to capture. They are at a developmental stage of becoming emerging adults, have likely spent a great deal of time as individuals connected with military life, and they should have agency in determining what types of support they need to thrive socially. The Youth Participatory Action Research (YPAR) model specifically ensures that student voices drive educational approaches to solving issues (Caraballo, Lozenski, Lyiscott, & Morrell, 2017). School psychologists can facilitate a YPAR process with military adolescents, who have the experience, developmental maturity, and agency to enact a plan to address social issues, including how best to engage socially with school settings into which they transition.

Facilitating Universal Social–Emotional and Behavioral Screening. As outlined in detail in Chapter 3 on the MTSS process adapted for military youth, school psychologists are instrumental in ensuring that the universal behavioral, social–emotional, and academic screening aspects of MTSS are inclusive of military youth, who may not be present when routine benchmark evaluations are completed. Ensuring that behavioral and social–emotional data are documented for adolescents is particularly critical, given that they may experience high rates of stress, and may be at an increased risk for depression and anxiety during the high school years as they think about their postsecondary plans. The opportunity to accumulate screening data as military youth reach the culminating years of formal schooling may also be one of the last times to identify them for additional social, behavioral, and mental health supports. In continuing to stress a strengths-based model of resiliency (Easterbrooks et al., 2013; Lerner et al., 2009, Masten, 2013b), capturing the data, described in Chapter 3, about military adolescents' perceptions of school climate and school connectedness is also recommended. School teams will then be in a better position to provide support to facilitate healthy social development and overall wellness with these amazing emerging young adults.

TABLE 4.2. Supportive Activities and Initiatives to Foster the Social Development of Military Children

Support/activity	Primary setting	Brief description	Link to more information
Operation Purple Camp	Summer camp setting in several states across the United States. You can click on a map that is posted on the "Link to more information."	Free 1-week camp for children connected with all uniformed services. Camps are offered for children ages 7–17, with some variability in ages served, depending on the camp location. Camps offer military youth a traditional overnight summer camp experience (arts, outdoor activities) and an opportunity to make friends with other military children.	*www.militaryfamily.org/programs/operation-purple/operation-purple-camp*
Operation Purple Buddy Camp	Summer camp setting in locations across the United States. There appear to be fewer buddy camps compared to Purple Camps. You can click on a map that is posted on the "Link to more information."	Free weekend summer camp for military-connected younger children (ages 5–8), modeled after Operation Purple Camp, in which they have a summer camp experience with an adult buddy (e.g., mom, dad, aunt, uncle).	*www.militaryfamily.org/programs/operation-purple/buddy-camp*
Boys and Girls Clubs of America (BGCA)	Local community-based BGCA organization or affiliate.	BGCA or one of its affiliated youth centers are located in all 50 states and 16 countries. BGCA has an outreach program specifically for military youth who can find a branch when relocating. BGCA offers free membership for military families to participating local BGCA clubs.	*www.bgca.org/about-us/military*
Military Kids Connect	Online military community with options for posting questions and messages and accessing video.	Recommended by Military One Source, Military Kids Connect is an online platform for military-connected youth to post messages on a message board and access videos produced by military youth on issues related to military life. The website features a segment (Dear DoC) where questions can be posed and answered by military youth.	*https://militarykidsconnect.dcoe.mil*

DoD summer camps	Camps offered directly or listed on the "Link to more information."	These camps are specifically for children who have a deployed parent or who are interested in an adventure camp. A search engine for summer activities that are located in the geographic region of one's military installation are also offered. *www.militaryonesource.mil/ family-relationships/family-life/ for-military-youth-and-teens/ department-of-defense-summer-camps*
Purple Up Month of the Military Child	Schools and educational institutions	The Department of Defense (DoD) established April as the month of the military child, in which a number of activities honor military-connected children, such as wearing purple on "Purple Up" day, hosting assemblies, and saluting military families at events (DoDEA, 2019a). The Month of the Military Child *www.dodea.edu/dodeaCelebrates/ Military-Child-Month.cfm*
Student 2 Student	Schools and educational institutions	An initiative of the MCEC, in which participating chapters pair Civilian students with military students to welcome them and facilitate their transition to a new school (MCEC, 2019a). There are three different types of Student 2 Student programs by grade level (elementary, middle, and high school). A map with active participating sites for each program is available on the MCEC website, here: *https:// www.militarychild.org/programs/student-2-student* *www.militarychild.org/programs/ student-2-student*
The Military Child Education Coalition (2019c) Ted Talks	Online and publicly accessible Ted Talks	One of the lessons features information about school transitions and the critical role of the first weeks of school. The Military Child Education Coalition (2019) Ted Talks in support of military youth are accessible at *https://ed.ted.com/on/0krz7o9g*

OVERALL SOCIAL DEVELOPMENT SUPPORTS FOR MILITARY YOUTH ACROSS THE DEVELOPMENTAL SPECTRUM AND CONCLUSIONS

Fostering the healthy social development of military youth is an important function for schools and school-based mental health professionals. Some of the developmental nuances that are part of the psychosocial development of all students, with adaptations for military youth, have been described. Thanks to the hard work of professional associations devoted specifically to military families, educators now have many sources of information to facilitate the social development of military youth across all developmental stages. Such resources and the ways to access them are found in Table 4.2. The focus has been specifically on sources that can facilitate social engagement, since military youth transition frequently to new communities and schools, and on events that honor them and raise their status in the school and with peers. Some of the resources and activities are specific to educational environments, whereas others are community based and provide socialization opportunities for military youth outside of traditional schools (e.g., Operation Purple Camp) (Buchanan, 2014). School-based mental health professionals and other educators have an essential role in fostering healthy social development among military youth in collaboration with military families, other adults, military role models, and the extended military community. There are many resources available to engage in this important work, based on the efforts of many, particularly those who have personally served in the military or who have family members who do so. Raising awareness of these resources and best practices in fostering healthy social development are important steps for educational professionals, who have the honor of working with this special group. More attention to systematic evaluations of how these efforts impact the social development and wellness of military youth is needed. School psychologists are ideally positioned to conduct such evaluations and to collect outcome data to inform and improve future efforts.

In conclusion, military youth are resilient and have enormous strengths (Park, 2011). They can greatly enhance any social environment and may simply need the right support and attention at the right time to do so. By facilitating transitions to new school environments and ongoing social supports, school psychologists can help military youth, who are already strong and resilient, to achieve the utmost of their potential and feel happy and connected in our schools. It is really a small task when we consider the enormous sacrifices that military youth and their families make to keep our country and the world safe.

CHAPTER 5

Delivery of Mental Health Supports

Consistent with other chapters, this chapter takes a resiliency and strengths-based approach to supporting the mental health and wellness of military youth and their families by honoring the many gifts and problem-solving skills they possess (Cozza et al., 2014; Lerner et al., 2009; Park, 2011). In addition, MTSS, described in detail in Chapter 3 (e.g., see Burns & Gibbons, 2012; Stoiber, 2014), are used as the organizing framework through which this approach can promote wellness and mental health among military youth (Astor et al., 2012). Mental health interventions tailored for military youth are described for each of the tiers, and an overview of special mental health considerations for military families and youth during a deployment cycle is provided. A case study of a family experiencing the tragic loss of their father and husband illustrates how MTSS, wraparound services (Bruns et al., 2004), the application of CBT Tier 2 and Tier 3 mental health interventions for complicated grief, and the coordination of community supports highlighted in this chapter could be implemented. Finally, the chapter concludes with a brief overview of the service delivery roles and activities that school psychologists and other mental health practitioners can engage in to support the mental health needs and wellness of military youth and their families within a continuum of mental health supports aligned with MTSS (NASP, 2015).

TIER 1/UNIVERSAL MENTAL HEALTH APPLICATIONS

Social Relationships and Connections

As described in the earlier chapters, cultivating an inviting, accepting, and welcoming school environment for all students, including military youth who may transition into a completely new school environment without knowing anyone, is vital. Research about military youth mental health risks and protective factors supports the utility of school psychologists working to ensure that all students have positive social connections and relationships as part of Tier 1 supports that, by definition, include military youth. For example, Lucier-Greer et al. (2015) evaluated the impact of several cumulative risk and protective factors among military adolescents living in one of four U.S. Army installations (one in Europe). They also wanted to know whether social relationships mediated the impact of the risk factors. A cumulative risk factor score was calculated, based on experiences such as feeling isolated, and military circumstances like numerous parental deployments, frequent school transitions, having more than one parent in the military, living far from a military installation, or being stationed outside of the United States. Protective factors were measured, including internal family support and engagement with formal Civilian or military programs, or religious institutions. As predicted, the cumulative risk index was associated with self-reported depression, weaker academic performance, and lower perceived persistence, whereas protective factors worked in the opposite direction. Adolescents with higher rates of family support and more social connections were less depressed, had stronger reported academic gains (i.e., grades), and were rated as more persistent. Of particular note is that social connections mediated, or lessened, the impact of cumulative risk factors on levels of self-reported depression, academic performance (grades), and persistence, whereas engagement in formal programs mediated academic areas only. The authors noted that although the measured protective factors did not completely eliminate the impact of cumulative risk factors on the measured outcomes, the presence of protective factors lessened their impact. These findings have implications for military youth living in military installations and in Civilian settings, because they document how strong social connections and engagement can have a positive impact on military youth and lessens the impact of risk factors. Therefore, school psychologists need to consider ways to create supportive school climates that foster social connections for all youth as part of Tier 1/universal supports.

A related study surveyed adolescents in four United States army installations (one in Europe) that had at least one active-duty parent (Lucier-Greer, Arnold, Mancini, Ford, & Bryant, 2016). Perceived adolescent well-being was assessed by a depression scale and several subscales that collectively evaluated adolescents' beliefs about the quality of their social relationships, family support, family problem-solving, access to guidance from others, and personal coping. Adolescents with an enlisted parent reported higher levels of depression, less social support/social integration, fewer close personal relationships (measured by Affectional Ties), and less perceived guidance from others, compared to adolescents who did not have an enlisted parent. As detailed by Lucier-Greer et al. (2016), explanations for these findings are complex. They note that enlisted military parents, who have a lower pay grade compared with officers, are also more likely to identify as racial minorities, work longer hours, and have children who attend public schools not on a military installation. Overall, enlisted military service members, compared with those of higher rank, have relatively fewer societal opportunities and less privilege (Booth et al., 2007, as cited in Lucier-Greer et al., 2016). Therefore, Lucier-Greer et al. caution against taking the findings about enlisted status as a deficit perspective about the families themselves. We concur with Lucier-Greer's interpretation and stress that the social development of military students is best supported by finding what works for them in making social connections, taking into account parents' busy lives and the daily sacrifices they make for the country's safety. There are many ways that schools can be accommodating in organizing social events for families that take into consideration work schedules and the busy lives of military families. Lucier-Greer et al. (2016) found that affectional ties were rated higher among youth who participated in military-sponsored activities, so school psychologists should be mindful of ways to facilitate such connections. Further, military youth who perceived that they had others to guide them were more likely to take part in military-sponsored activities; adolescents who had frequent school changes had lower self-reported guidance. These findings show the importance of adult mentors positioned in/connected with the school to facilitate these opportunities for social engagement of military students. This study also underscores that getting involved in activities depends on obtaining the proper guidance and being sensitive to the work/family balance that military families must navigate, particularly enlisted families who will not be likely to have as many resources and flexibility compared with higher-ranking service members. Children and adolescents, but particularly military youth who frequently find themselves in new school settings, will benefit from intentional universal/Tier 1 social supports and relationship building so they are comfortable accepting and seeking guidance. They will also benefit from having sensitive and empathic mental health professionals who can advocate for flexibility. It is also important to listen to families and determine what types of social supports they would like to partake in, as well as how accommodations for military youth and families can be made in logistics and timing, so that they can participate and feel supported.

Based on the combined findings of these two studies, delivering universal/Tier 1 supports, as described in Chapter 3, and building schoolwide systems that prioritize social connections and inclusiveness in activities (Lucier-Greer et al., 2015; Lucier-Greer et al., 2016) for all students in a school system including military youth, are critical components of foundational supports. Relationships are critical for all students, but based on the research of Lucier-Greer et al. (2015, 2016), they may serve as buffers that mediate the cumulative risk factors that may make military youth subject to mental health concerns. The Tier 1 social development strategies described in Chapter 4 and the related interventions in Table 4.2, such as making sure that military youth are socially supported when they transition to new schools and recognizing the invaluable contributions they and their families make, are useful. We highlight some special considerations for building social connections and facilitating the involvement of military youth in school activities:

- School psychologists need to be mindful of the type of educational context they are working in when facilitating social relationships with military youth. Chapter 2 described the primary school contexts where military youth are educated (e.g., Civilian schools, DoD schools, and non-DoD schools in international settings), and these varied settings have important implications for the opportunities and the types of social engagement military youth may likely be exposed to. School psychologists in public school environments who work with youth who do not live near military installations need to be particularly cognizant of ways to encourage their participation in school-related activities, and to remain sensitive to the demands of military life. Of the nearly 2 million youth who have one or more parents in the military, over 80% attend U.S. public schools, and fewer than 8% are in DoD schools (Military Child Education Coalition, n.d.). Therefore, the types of military-related social engagement described by Lucier-Greer et al. (2016) may not be available to the majority of military youth.

- In addition, the most recent military conflicts are fought solely by an all-volunteer military force consisting of members of the National Guard and Reserves who are not connected to a military base (Sheppard, Malatras, & Israel, 2010) and are least likely to be connected to other military families. School psychologists need to be particularly mindful of identifying these youth, since they are not a subgroup who are required to be tracked through ESSA (See Chapter 7 on legislation that affects military youth). These youth may need special attention to ensure that they are made to feel welcomed and made part of the school community.

- As described in Chapter 4 on healthy social development, school personnel in public school environments could arrange military-focused groups for these students so that there is an opportunity for individuals who have similar experiences to interact with one another and feel connected. In addition, as also discussed in Chapter 4, schools can serve as anchors for honoring and welcoming military youth through assemblies and educating not only school personnel, but also the entire student body about the sacrifices made by those who serve in the military (DoD, 2015).

- School psychologists can also collect and analyze data about the percentage of students in school who participate in at least one club or sports activity to evaluate school connectedness among all students and disaggregate these data that apply to military youth (American Association of School Administrators, 2009a; Centers for Disease Control and Prevention, 2009). Additional data could be collected on the number of students who believe that there is an adult in the building they can reach out to with a problem or issue, which is a question on the Schoolwide Evaluation Tool (SET; Horner et al., 2004), a measure used to assess Schoolwide Positive Behavior Support (SWPBS) implementation status at the universal/Tier 1 level (Lewis et al., 2010). These data can be connected with the types of data described in Chapter 2 on MTSS systems of universal social–emotional and behavioral screening.

School Climate

Connected with intentional efforts to ensure that both non-military and military-connected students have access to positive social relationships and connections, the building of an overall accepting and welcoming school climate is an important component of Tier 1 mental health supports. Specific to military youth, De Pedro et al. (2015) evaluated the findings from the California Healthy Kids Survey (CHKS: Austin et al. 2013a; Austin et al. 2013b) that was conducted in six military-connected California school districts. The survey was administered to 7th-, 9th-, and 11th-grade military and non-military students, and included items that assessed school climate and additional items specifically developed for military youth (Gilreath et al., 2014; see DePedro et al. [2015] for the full findings of their logistic regression). Deployment status, particularly having two or more family deployments, was a significant predictor for depression and suicidal ideation. Moreover, students with a sibling in the military had higher rates of self-reported depression and suicidal ideation compared with peers who had a parent in the military and those with no military connection at all. When added to the regression model, school climate components impacted self-reported well-being, depression, and suicidal ideation. For example, caring and meaningful relationships were associated with a greater likelihood of higher self-reported well-being. Surprisingly, meaningful participation was associated with higher self-reported depressive symptoms, but as expected, it was associated with lower suicidal ideation. Higher self-reported feelings of safety were associated with lower levels of self-reported depression and suicidal ideation and reports of greater well-being. In addition, school connectedness was associated with lower self-reports of depression and suicidal ideation. These findings are quite promising in making the case that school climate, as a Tier 1 support, can alleviate the stressors of military-connected students. Of particular note, when school climate variables were added to the regression model, a family member's military status as active duty or not appeared to have dropped out of the equation. In particular, feelings of safety, school connectedness, and meaningful and positive relationships are important components of building an accepting school climate as part of Tier 1 supports. School psychologists should take an active role in encouraging positive relationships and school safety among all students, inclusive of military youth, as part of important foundational supports.

Universal and Classroom-Based Social–Emotional Learning Approaches

Another important component of Tier 1 universal mental and behavioral health supports is the direct teaching of positive coping and emotional regulation skills as components of social–emotional learning (SEL). The state of Illinois, where the author works as a school psychology faculty member, was the first state to adopt Social and Emotional Learning Standards, with goals for instruction that are developmental in nature (Illinois State Board of Education, n.d.). The first goal links specifically to identifying and managing emotions and behavior, which could be a framework for schoolwide teaching of effective coping and regulation of emotions to alleviate everyday stressors. Schoolwide SEL supports by definition include military youth and could serve as a resiliency buffer to mitigate the unique stressors that they encounter (Morris & Age, 2009). SEL instruction could be paired with the implementations of universal behavioral supports, such as SWPBS (McIntosh & Goodman, 2016), outlined in Chapter 3 on MTSS.

Collaborative for Academic, Social, and Emotional Learning (CASEL)

School psychologists have access to evidence-supported SEL programs that have been well researched and are described in detail. For example, CASEL has developed comprehensive guides that feature evidence-based social–emotional programs (CASEL, 2012; 2015). Each program was required to meet CASEL-identified standards, which included the following: (1) at least one controlled study (e.g., comparison group or pre–post assessment); (2) a positive impact on academics and/or behavioral, social–emotional learning content aligned with CASE-identified standards; and (3) evidence of training and support (CASEL, 2012). The CASEL 2012 guide has evidence-based social–emotional learning programs for use in classrooms at the preschool and elementary level. The CASEL 2015 Middle and High School Edition for middle and high school students differentiates between programs that are "SELect" (CASEL, 2015, p. 11), "complementary" (CASEL, 2015, p. 11), and "promising" (CASEL, 2015, p. 12). The "SELect" program designation, the most rigorous CASEL endorsement, is given to programs that not only show scientific evidence of effective behavioral and/or academic outcomes, but also provide professional development and ongoing technical support as part of implementation across several years. The "complementary" designation is given to programs that meet the CASEL-designated research criteria but are not comprehensive enough to be stand-alone SEL programs. Instead, these are recommended by CASEL to be used in conjunction with other comprehensive SEL programs. Finally, the "promising" designation is given to programs that do not yet meet scientific research criteria, but are well constructed and comprehensive models of SEL programs.

Military youth in schools that deliver an SEL curriculum will have access to these supports on a system-wide and classroom basis. Schools that provide SEL along with behavioral supports (McIntosh & Goodman, 2016) will establish a strong foundation for developing problem-solving, emotional regulation, and coping skills. These skills have been identified in the military research as supporting a strengths-based resiliency perspective that can buffer the mental health stressors that military youth are at risk for and/or may experience (Lucier-Greer et al., 2015; Lucier-Greer et al., 2016).

As with implementing other Tier 1 supports and the universal screening described elsewhere (and particularly Chapter 3), school psychologists need to be mindful of whether military youth are present to receive such supports, given the number of times their families relocate. Therefore, school psychologists should work to the maximum extent possible to ensure that military youth receive SEL supports as they transition in. This may require adaptations to the way that the curriculum and interventions are delivered. The following are some ways in which the SEL curriculum and/or interventions could be adapted to make sure that military youth receive access to these important supports.

- Provide additional SEL instruction to military youth in small groups if they have missed universal and/or classroom-based instruction.
- When feasible, additional systemwide SEL supports can be provided, which would benefit both military and non-military youth.

- SEL instruction can be creatively infused into classroom lessons using peer grouping and small-group instruction. As an example, a school psychologist could consult with a classroom teacher to provide SEL instruction in skills that military youth and their families have developed as part of military life, such as resiliency, flexibility, and adaptability. Military youth could serve as leaders in classroom instruction on these topics. There may also be skills that they would like help in developing, and lessons could be structured to serve this purpose.

ADDRESSING THE SPECIALIZED NEEDS OF MILITARY YOUTH: TIER 2 AND TIER 3 APPLICATIONS

In addition to establishing a foundation of Tier 1 supports that focus on positive relationships and an inviting school climate and teaching social–emotional skills to military youth, school psychologists need to be knowledgeable about supplemental/secondary (Tier 2) and individualized tertiary (Tier 3) mental health supports for military youth and their families. School psychologists and other school mental health providers may be the only professionals who recognize the mental health risk factors among military youth whose families either may not have easy access to these services, such as those in the National Guard or Reserves (Sheppard et al., 2010), or be in a position to actively pursue them outside of a school context. Military families may be hesitant to seek mental health services owing to a perceived or a real impact on the service member(s)' career or mental health stigma (Campbell, Brown, & Okwara, 2011). Although more is being done to eradicate the stigma attached to mental health issues and increase access to services among military families, there are often unaddressed mental health concerns that schools can help to support. For example, PTSD is a mental health concern common to service members that can affect the entire family unit (Leen-Feldner et al., 2013, as cited in Hisle-Gorman et al., 2015; Seal et al., 2009, as cited in Kaplow, Layne, Saltzman, Cozza, & Pynoos, 2013). Although military service members and their families are ever resilient, stressors of military life may also make military youth more susceptible to mental health problems (Friedberg & Brelsford, 2011). During times of deployment, youth and their families also may be more at risk for mental health issues because there may be higher rates of abuse and domestic violence (Campbell et al., 2011). Military families may also be devastated when a service member dies as a result of combat or non-combat related military action, by suicide, or when they witness a very serious injury (Cohen & Mannarino, 2011; Hisle-Gorman et al., 2015; Kaplow et al., 2013). Therefore, knowing how to effectively respond, select, or deliver Tier 2 and/or Tier 3 interventions when warranted with military youth and their families is critical (Campbell et al., 2011; Friedberg & Brelsford, 2011). To this end, an overview of evidence-supported Tier 2 and/or Tier 3 interventions that can be put into practice and/or adapted to support their mental health and wellness is provided next.

Cognitive-Behavioral Interventions

Cognitive-Behavioral Therapy with Internalizing Disorders, Stress, and Trauma

Depression and anxiety are internalizing mental health disorders that military youth experience (Chandra et al., 2011; Flake et al., 2009). However, these disorders are less likely to be detected, and therefore treated, compared to externalizing behavior disorders (Huberty, 2012; Tandon, Cardeli, & Luby, 2009). Cognitive-behavioral therapy (CBT) has a well-established track record for success in treating a wide variety of internalizing and externalizing disorders among children and adolescents from a variety of backgrounds (Allen, 2011; Friedberg & McClure, 2015). Although more research is needed about the applications of CBT to military youth (Campbell et al., 2011), CBT remains the treatment of choice in addressing numerous mental health concerns of this population (Friedberg & Brelsford, 2011; Kaplow et al., 2013). For example, when writing about the ways to support the mental health needs of military youth facing family deployments, Friedberg &. Brelsford (2011) recommend the use of CBT, owing to the evidence for effectively treating depression, anxiety, and significant stress. The authors also point to the practicality of implementing CBT modules in real-world environments. We concur that CBT has promise, as it is particularly adaptable for schools that military children attend and where school psychologists have the expertise to implement mental health interventions. In terms of specific CBT interventions, Friedberg and Brelsford (2011) recommend the Penn Resiliency Program (Gillham, Reivich, & Jaycox, 2008; Reivich & Shatte, 2002, as cited in Friedberg & Brelsford, 2011) for military youth, in part, because of the program's focus on resiliency. Resiliency is a hallmark of military youth (Friedberg & Brelsford, 2011; Park, 2011) and is consistent with the strengths-based focus of this book. Based on many years of randomized clinical trial studies, the Penn Resiliency Program demonstrates effectiveness in treating anxiety, depression and adjustment issues (Brunwasser, Gillham, & Kim, 2009; Gillham, Hamilton, Freres, Patton, & Gallup, 2006). Although controlled applied research applications of the Penn Resiliency Program for military youth in schools may not yet exist, a review of information on the University of Pennsylvania Positive Psychology Web (*https://ppc.sas.upenn.edu/services/resilience-training-army*) shows extensive resiliency training of Army service members, Army Civilian personnel, and their families. Through a train-the-trainer model, Army personnel teach fellow soldiers about resiliency. Table 5.1 provides a summary of the Penn Resiliency Program.

CBT in the Treatment of Traumatic Grief

It is a sad reality that military youth may face not only long absences of parents, siblings, and other relatives because of extended deployments, but the reality of injury and death of a loved military family member. When the unspeakable happens, school psychologists can play a vital role in dispensing needed support, provided that they are familiar with the various types of grief and how to identify the signs of traumatic grief that require specialized treatments. This information is also important to share with family members and colleagues, particularly teachers, who may require psychoeducation to understand how best to help students who are coping with a traumatic event or in the throes of a military deployment and reintegration cycle. Cohen and Mannarino (2011) distinguish between two types of grief reactions in children: adaptive grief versus traumatic grief. In traumatic grief, children may have intrusive images of their loved one's death and the circumstances surrounding it and may fill in unknown or unclear information about the death. As a result of these intrusive images, children and adolescents avoid thinking about the death and the loved one they have lost (Cohen & Mannarino, 2011). Therefore, youth experiencing traumatic grief may not be emotionally ready to partake in the tradition of honoring the service member at a formal military funeral or participate in their family's religious or cultural observances (Cohen & Mannarino, 2011). When the reactions of military youth, such as avoiding prescribed rituals or not speaking of the deceased loved one, are misunderstood, family members may become even angrier during a highly stressful time in their lives (Cohen & Mannarino 2011). Similarly, teachers and other school personnel may not understand the avoidant reactions of their students and how best to support them.

Similar to recommended treatments for internalizing disorders, variations grounded in CBT are offered as an evidence-supported response to traumatic grief with military families (Cohen & Mannarino, 2011; Kaplow et al., 2013). Cohen and Mannarino recommend the use of trauma-focused CBT (TF-CBT; Cohen et al., 2010, as cited in Cohen & Mannarino, 2011) to address traumatic grief issues because it focuses on addressing challenges faced by military youth, particularly faulty cognitions, and emphasizes teaching coping strategies to help with modulation of affect (Morris & Age, 2009). Cohen and Mannarino (2011) also share valuable resources that can be useful for school psychologists, who can make referrals for military families to attend grief camps that are based on CBT principles and offer bereaved military youth a peer support system; one such resource is the Tragedy Assistance Program for Survivors (TAPS) Good Grief Program for Bereaved Military Children. Brief summaries of TF-CBT and TAPS Good Grief Camps are included in Table 5.1.

Kaplow and colleagues (2013) recommend the use of a related approach, Multidimensional Grief Theory (Layne, Saltzman, Kaplow, & Pynoos, 2013; Pynoos, Layne, & Kaplow, 2012), as a way of conceptualizing and treating traumatic grief among service members who have experienced the loss of a comrade and among military youth who are grieving the death of their parent or other family member. Given the lack of attention to grief reactions in children and adolescents in the literature, Kaplow et al. (2013) advocate for Multidimensional Grief Theory as a developmentally based model of grief (Layne et al., 2013; Pynoos et al., 2012). In their explanation of the theory, they differentiate between components of grief that include separation distress (e.g., missing a deceased person, engaging in the destructive behaviors of the deceased person, or remaining stagnant in the same developmental stage as at the time the person died), existential- and/or identity-related distress (e.g., disruptions to self-identity, taking on unplanned adult roles that interfere with life plans and life satisfaction), and distress about the death circumstances, particularly if it was violent and/or if the grieving person directly witnessed the threat or death (Pynoos, 1992, as cited in Kaplow et al., 2013). The grief reaction may also be expressed differently depending on the developmental stage and internal characteristics of the military youth, as well as the broader social context and culture in which the youth functions (Pynoos, Steinberg, & Wraith, 1995, as cited in Kaplow et al., 2013). Similar to Cohen and Mannerino's (2011) descriptions of how adaptive grief differs from traumatic grief, Kaplow et al.'s (2013) Multidimensional Grief Theory (Layne et al., 2013; Pynoos et al., 2012) explains how normal adaptive grief might morph into maladaptive grief via maladaptive coping strategies. A critical point made in Kaplow et al. (2013) is that school psychologists who focus primarily or exclusively on PTSD in the absence of grief may end up with a limited understanding of the issues that guide treatment. Kaplow et al. (2013) state,

> Returning service members' reactions to trauma reminders versus loss reminders may have different consequences for children and other family members living in the home . . . focusing exclusively or even primarily on PTSD in returning service members may thus miss important concepts. (p. 331)

Kaplow et al. (2013) further emphasize the need to consider not only the traditional trauma signs, but also loss reminders among returning service members who may benefit from participating, with their families in cognitive behavioral conjoint therapy, which incorporates PTSD psychoeducation and focuses on family interpersonal relationships (Monson & Fredman, 2012, as cited in Kaplow et al., 2013). In addition, to fully understand a youth's grief, Kaplow et al. (2013) emphasize the importance of knowing the circumstances surrounding a parental combat death, which can occur following the frequent separations in long deployments and therefore might seem less real. Furthermore, interpersonal conflict about some parents surviving and others not surviving and the need to move off base within a year of a service member's death are additional issues to consider in these times of extreme stress (Kaplow et al., 2013).

Interventions and activities that align with addressing the grief dimensions outlined by Multidimensional Grief Theory (Layne et al., 2013; Pynoos et al., 2012) include creating positive memories of the deceased through scrapbooking and thinking about ways to continue the person's legacy (Kaplow et al., 2013). Separation distress can be targeted by imagining positive images of the deceased service member, and circumstance-related distress can be minimized by informing the youth about the death details in a developmentally appropriate manner (Kaplow et al., 2013). In terms of group supports, Layne et al. (2013) developed a manualized group-delivered grief and trauma program for adolescents called the Trauma and Grief Component Therapy for Adolescents (TGCTA; Cox et al., 2007; Layne et al., 2013, as cited in Kaplow et al., 2013; Saltzman et al., 2003), which is based on the three dimensions of grief in Multidimensional Grief Theory (Layne et al., 2013; Pynoos et al., 2012). TGCTA is a well-researched group and/or individual intervention that has been implemented and evaluated numerous times within varied treatment settings (e.g., school districts, juvenile justice settings, community settings in clinics) in national and international contexts employing rigorous designs, including a randomized control trial (Layne et al., 2008). More recently, TGCTA is offered in a modular format that can be implemented in schools with flexibility at the classroom, group, or individual level (Saltzman et al., 2017). A summary of TGCTA is provided in Table 5.1.

TIER 3 INTENSIVE SUPPORTS: WRAPAROUND PLANNING

As described briefly in Chapter 2, for military families and youth with the most intensive needs, wraparound planning (Bruns et al., 2004) and the coordination of supports across settings, including schools, community groups, and other youth and family-serving agencies (Adelman & Taylor, 2012), could be facilitated by school psychologists and other school-based mental health professionals. For example, family members with significant psychiatric and related mental health issues run the risk of interacting with multiple agencies that are not coordinated with one another, adding to the significant stress that these families may already experience (Adelman & Taylor, 2012). School psychologists can help to organize a wraparound planning team that includes individuals who are critical to maintaining family stability in the wake of multiple concurrent stressors, such as relocations and deployments, and during tragic events, such as combat injuries and death (Bruns et al., 2004). The specific Tier 2 and/or Tier 3 interventions for trauma situations featured in Table 5.1 can also be helpful in wraparound planning. A wraparound team should include the central people in a family's life chosen by the family members, not individuals who are traditionally part of mental health teams, such as professionals (Bruns et al., 2004). The military family can designate natural supports important to them, such as people who help with day-to-day routines as well as with military deployments and family moves (Bruns et al., 2004). The family may call upon extended family members, such as grandparents, aunts, and close friends within and outside of the military.

MILITARY DEPLOYMENTS: SPECIAL CONSIDERATIONS FOR SCHOOL PSYCHOLOGISTS

In this section, we focus on mental health and wellness considerations with military families and youth in the throes of a military deployment cycle. Specialized attention may be warranted and to the degree possible, we recommend that supports are delivered within the MTSS tiered framework that is available in the school. However, the unique factors related to each family's experiences and support systems during military deployment should be considered on a case-by-case basis to determine, with the family, how best to be helpful. School psychologists will not want to automatically assume that all military families experiencing a deployment or its aftermath will respond in an identical way or have a diagnosable mental health condition requiring intervention. This would undermine a strengths-based approach with military families and youth that honors their resilience in coping with mental health and social–emotional issues. Still, it is important to recognize that military deploy-

TABLE 5.1. Tier 2 (Group) and/or Tier 3 (Individual) CBT-Based Mental Health Interventions for Military Youth and Families

Program/intervention (authors)	Brief description and treatment format	Target group and research outcomes	Link to more information and resources
Penn Resilience Program (Reivich & Shatte, 2002, as cited in Friedberg & Brelsford, 2011)	A group-level cognitive-behavioral intervention used to treat anxiety and depression with a focus on challenging inaccurate thoughts and problem solving. Grounded in the theoretical orientations of Albert Ellis, Aaron Beck, and Martin Seligman. Delivered in 12 90-minute lessons or 18–24 60-minute lessons	Middle childhood. As reported on the program's website, approximately 20 controlled studies, most incorporating a randomized controlled trial. Positive findings for reductions in depression and anxiety (some mixed results). Follow-up studies show sustained effects, 2 or more years out. See the following link for publications (some with links to access the studies): *https://ppc.sas.upenn.edu/empirical-evaluations-prp*	University of Pennsylvania Positive Psychology Center website: *https://ppc.sas.upenn.edu* Description of the program: *https://ppc.sas.upenn.edu/research/resilience-children* Description of the lessons: *https://ppc.sas.upenn.edu/sites/default/files/prplessons.pdf*
Trauma-focused cognitive-behavioral therapy (TF-CBT; Cohen & Mannarino, 2011; Cohen, Mannarino, & Deblinger, 2010; Cohen, Mannarino, & Cozza, 2014)	Treatment manual provides clinicians with guidance to apply TF-CBT with military families. The manual illustrates ways to adapt TF-CBT to traumas and grief experienced by military families, such as deployment-related trauma,	Treatment manual has a family and an individual child focus, with examples for each. TF-CBT has a well-established literature base, including many randomized controlled national and international trials.	Cohen and colleagues recommend that clinicians have basic grounding in TF-CBT, which can be supported by taking the online course TF-CBT web 2.0 (*https://tfcbt2.musc.edu/en*) offered through the Medical University of South Carolina (2017)

	military family injury/death, and domestic violence and abuse. Short vignettes or scenarios using military family examples are illustrated throughout.	See National Child Traumatic Stress Network (2012) fact sheet (*www.nctsn.org/sites/default/files/interventions/tfcbt_fact_sheet.pdf*).	The Trauma-Focused CBT National Therapist Certification Program (2020) has a webpage—Trauma-Focused CBT Military Implementation Resources—with handouts for parents and caregivers specific to military youth experiencing traumatic grief: *https://tfcbt.org/tf-cbt-military-implementation-resources*.
Tragedy Assistance Program for Survivors (TAPS) Good Grief Camps	A camp experience for military children to process grief following the loss of a military family member; a military mentor is assigned, and separate programming is available for surviving parents (TAPS, n. d.)	Children, adolescents, and their families who have lost a military service member	The TAPS website has more information about the program's offerings: *www.taps.org/youthprograms*
Trauma and grief component therapy for adolescents (TGCTA; Layne et al., 2013, as cited in Kaplow et al., 2013; Saltzman et al., 2017)	A group-level intervention that has been adapted from the three dimensions of grief espoused by Multidimensional Grief Theory (Layne et al., 2013; Pynoos et al., 2011).	Youth and their families who have lost a service member. The more recently published version of TGCTA is presented in modular format and offers a structured treatment protocol with lessons and well-researched assessment tools developed by the authors (Saltzman et al., 2017).	The National Child Traumatic Stress Network (2018) provides a detailed fact sheet about TGCTA on its website at *www.nctsn.org/sites/default/files/interventions/tgcta_fact_sheet.pdf*

ments are one potential risk factor for mental health concerns and a potential stressor that school psychologists will want to keep on their radar (Sheppard et al., 2010).

Deployment Characteristics and Family/Youth Mental Health

Military Service Branch

It is also important to take into account the branch of service military families are enlisted in, as this factor impacts not only the nature of the deployment, but also the support received from other military families facing similar situations and their level of access to mental health services. In the last several years, volunteer active-duty National Guard and Reservists have experienced deployments of the longest duration and the highest number of repeated deployments since World War II (Esposito-Smythers et al., 2011; Fenning et al., 2013). National Guard and Reservists deployed during the recent Iraq and Afghanistan conflicts may be particularly at risk for a lack of community and understanding, potentially as a result of having experienced multiple and sustained deployments, and not typically being stationed on a military base or living in Civilian communities (Mansfield et al., 2010, as cited in Esposito-Smythers et al., 2011). Therefore, National Guard and Reservists may not have the same access to services as active-duty military personnel or live near others who are familiar with military life and culture (Mansfield et al., 2010, as cited in Esposito-Smythers et al., 2011; Siegel, Davis, the Committee on Psychosocial Aspects of Child and Family Functioning and Section on Uniformed Services, 2013; Werber et al., 2013). School psychologists should be particularly mindful of the mental health needs of military families in the National Guard and Reserves for these reasons. Outreach may be called for to determine whether mental health and wellness supports would be warranted at school and/or whether referrals to community mental health or other support systems would help these families.

Regardless of branch of service, Sheppard et al. (2010) also note that if the deployment of the service member is with a different military unit than the assigned one, then military family members may not have the same level of support as if a deployment is occurring within one's own military unit. School psychologists need to educate themselves and extend psychoeducation to colleagues to better understand these nuances of deployment, particularly among those who have not themselves served in the military or worked extensively with military families. It is clear that "one size does not fit all" in terms of the nature of the deployment and the individual situation of each military family.

Factors Related to Length of Deployment, Combat-Related Deployment, and Injuries

The length of deployment is an important factor to consider when thinking about the potential impact it has on the wellness and mental health of military family members. Lester and colleagues (2010) interviewed the non-deployed caregivers and/or the active-duty Army or Marine Corps military parents with children between the ages of 6–17. One parent was either deployed at the time of the study or had recently returned from combat in Afghanistan and Iraq. Parental reported distress and the total cumulative length of combat-related deployments independently predicted childhood depression and externalizing behaviors. In addition, anxiety was elevated in children with parents who were currently deployed or had recently returned from combat.

The deployment of a service member is compounded when a tragic injury or even death occurs, either in combat or through another means (e.g., friendly fire, suicide attempt or completion). Traumatic brain injuries are particularly prevalent as a result of the Iraqi and Afghanistan conflicts (Sammons & Batten, 2008, as cited in Sheppard et al., 2010). The clinical diagnosis of PTSD is particularly stressful for parents and presents parenting challenges (Chandra, Burns, Tanilelian, Jaycox, & Scott, 2008, as cited in Sogomonyan & Cooper, 2010; Sheppard et al., 2010).

Assessments of Emotional and Behavioral Concerns in Deployment Situations

Chandra et al. (2011) conducted one of the most comprehensive surveys through phone interviews with military parents and youth about their behavioral and emotional health, which included 12-month follow-up data. The sample was taken from applicants to Operation Purple Camp (National Military Family Association, n.d.). All youth had a parent who had been deployed. Based on the Strengths and Difficulties Questionnaire (SDQ: Goodman, 1997), 30% of caregivers rated their children as having moderate-to-high levels of emotional and behavioral difficulties at baseline, with a significant decrease from baseline to 12 months, yet an increase at 6 months, compared with the final ratings. All ratings were clinically elevated relative to a community normative SDQ sample. The military youth's self-report on the SDQ showed similar clinical elevations relative to community peers, but there were significant reductions in these concerns over time, as 44% of youth reported moderate-to-high levels of concerns on the SDQ at baseline, compared to 38% at the 12-month mark (relative to 19% in the normative community comparative sample). In addition, youth who reported difficulty communicating with the nondeployed parent were more likely to have self-described emotional challenges. The youth participants reported no significant concerns with respect to peer relationships, but did report significant difficulties with family functioning based on the Pediatric Quality of Life Inventory (PedsQL; Varni, Burwinkle, & Seid, 2006). The reader is referred to Chandra et al. (2011) for the complete analysis and study findings.

Risk of Child Maltreatment

Hisle-Gorman and colleagues (2015) compared Military Health Care system visits from 2006 to 2007 for mental and/or behavioral health, child maltreatment, and injuries among children ages 3–8 of soldiers who were deployed, deployed and injured, or not deployed. They found that mental and behavioral health visits, as well as visits for injuries and child maltreatment were higher among children of deployed parents as well as children whose parents were injured in combat compared to children whose parents had not experienced a deployment. Mental and behavioral health visits among children whose parents had experienced both a deployment and a combat-related injury were the highest among all three groups, with an 82% higher rate among those whose parents were injured and deployed, compared to those whose parents were not deployed, and a 67% higher rate in relation to those whose parents experienced a deployment, but were not injured.

These findings are significant for school psychologists who may be one of the few school-based mental health professionals who interact with children of deployed and/or injured service members. With parental consent, they can collaborate with military health care systems and local primary health care providers to ensure that young children's needs and those of their families are being met throughout all stages of the deployment cycle. The Hisle-Gorman et al. (2015) study includes young preschool children who are understudied in the military literature and might be overlooked. For this younger group of children, school psychologists who engage in routine early childhood screenings (U.S. Department of Education, 2008) could add screening questions about recent deployments, combat-related injuries, and other military service issues as part of the process, which would pick up individuals from a wider net in each community.

Family Stressors and Dynamics across the Deployment Cycle

The available research also guides our understanding of the impact of the deployment cycle on military family and youth stressors. Esposito-Smythers et al. (2011) describe the deployment phase as being potentially marked by stress for the nondeployed parent owing to increased child care and related responsibilities and changes in family boundaries and roles. They also note a potential absence of understanding of these stressors among community members who are unfamiliar with the difficulties of military life. Esposito-Smythers et al. (2011) note that the postdeployment and reintegration phase of deployment may be marked by reestablishing the family roles and responsibilities assumed in the deployed parent's absence. The roles may involve shifts in family dynamics, including issues such as the loyalty that a child may have toward the nondeployed parent or the degree of reliance and involvement of care networks used during the deployment phase. In addition, worry about the physical and emotional health of the deployed service member and the next deployment may be evident during transition to postdeployment (Chandra et al., 2011, as cited in Esposito-Smythers et al., 2011).

In related research, Flake and colleagues (2009) conducted a study of parenting stress among army spouses living in a military installation with a deployed partner and elementary-age children. Based on the Parenting Stress Index (PSI; Cohen, Kamarck, & Mermelstein, 1983), 32% of parents rated their children as high risk on the tool, compared to 13% of the national normative sample. In addition, using the Pediatric Symptom Checklist (PSC), 39% rated their children in the clinically elevated rating for internalizing symptoms, and over 56% indicated that their children had trouble sleeping (Jellinek et al., 1988). In terms of parenting stress, 42% of the sample noted high levels of stress, which was significantly greater than a normative comparison sample. Based on modeling techniques, perceptions of parental stress and a lack of military support were the strongest predictors of high ratings for childhood psychosocial problems. Specific types of support, such as church support, non-military and military organization support, and overall general community support strongly predicted psychosocial functioning.

To add to this literature, Huebner, Mancini, Wilcox, Grass, and Grass (2007) held focus groups with adolescents participating in a camp for military youth with a deployed parent, mostly to combat zones, about their deployment perspectives. Among other findings (see Huebner et al., 2007), adolescents had ambiguous feelings about their changing roles while the deployed service member was gone, such as having additional adult roles and responsibilities, not having as much time for extracurricular and leisure activities, and then adjusting once again to old roles and responsibilities when the military parent returned. In terms of mental health concerns, participants made a number of statements about deployment, such as saying that they had feelings of depression and sadness, as well as sleeping and eating problems. Finally, participants noted more interpersonal conflict, such as arguing and yelling in benign situations, and noted changes in the tolerance and stress levels of the parent who remained at home, usually their mother. The adolescents also described problems in redeveloping and/or restoring the relationship with the deployed service member upon returning home.

Support for Military Families and Youth Experiencing Deployment

Sheppard et al. (2010) note that family stability, using a definition created by Israel, Roderick, and Ivanova (2002), may mediate the role of deployment on child outcomes and serve as a protective factor. Israel et al. (2002) distinguish between global family stability and molecular family stability (Israel et al., 2002, as cited in Sheppard et al., 2010). Global family stability centers on major life events, such as divorce, death, and relocations, whereas molecular family stability concerns familiar routines and a sense of predictability, as well as activities that occur outside of the home, but require family involvement (Israel et al., 2002, as cited in Sheppard et al., 2010). Sheppard and colleagues (2010) further note that molecular family stability may be connected to parenting skills. School psychologists can facilitate prevention-oriented interventions and psychoeducational groups for military families and youth within schools and in collaboration with community agencies that help them and their extended family since they are proven protective factors that mediate mental health outcomes and wellness (Lester et al., 2012; Lester et al., 2013; Lucier-Greer et al., 2015; Lucier-Greer et al., 2016).

Two highly researched and applied interventions specifically targeting parenting skills—the After Deployment Adaptive Parenting Tools (ADAPT) program (Gewirtz et al., 2009) and Families OverComing Under Stress (FOCUS; Garcia et al., 2015)—could be implemented with families and would specifically support family stability as a mediator of deployment on military youth and family mental health outcomes. (Refer to Table 3.2

for a comparison of these two interventions and related online resources.) Briefly, ADAPT (Gewirtz et al., 2009) focuses specifically on parenting skills and readjustment following a deployment, and FOCUS emphasizes family resilience, emotional regulation, problem solving, goal setting, and managing trauma reminders, which has relevance for the stressors and traumatic events experienced during deployments.

The Tier 1 supports described earlier in this chapter would be especially beneficial for military youth and families who are experiencing the stress of deployment. They may benefit as well from access to additional embedded Tier 1 and/or Tier 2 curricula and interventions, such as relaxation training as a compliment, for example, to the Tier 2 cognitive behavioral interventions. It can be argued that deployment situations do not necessarily call for a set protocol or action, but they are certainly experiences that school psychologists and other educators need to be sensitive to. They need to listen to military family members, and approach their efforts by respecting their strengths. School psychologists also need to be vigilant and mindful about facilitating the delivery of any social–emotional and mental health prevention and intervention that they deserve during a potentially challenging time. The following fictional case study features the same schools described in the Chapter 3 case study (Allen Middle School and Meadowood Elementary), and discusses the experiences of the Spencer Family. You may wish to review the case study description of these schools in Chapter 3, which features the universal academic screening and schoolwide data collection efforts related to school climate and bullying.

CASE EXAMPLE OF INDIVIDUALIZED FAMILY SUPPORTS IN MEADOWOOD ELEMENTARY AND ALLEN MIDDLE SCHOOL

The Spencer family includes Jennifer (mother); Dahlia (daughter, age 8, at Meadowood Elementary); and Amy (daughter, age 13. at Allen Middle School). They recently experienced the loss of (Ryan, husband and father), who died 9 months ago during a deployment in Afghanastan from a handmade explosive device detonating during a mission. There was initially limited information about the circumstances surrounding the tragedy. After several months, details emerged that the explosion happened when Ryan was riding in a convoy in the area with three comrades. Ryan and a comrade were seriously injured at the time and later died after receiving treatment for their injuries. The two other comrades suffered signficant injuries, one of whom lost a leg, but both survived the traumatic event. The tragedy occurred during Ryan's second deployment, when he and his family had just received news that he was about to be sent home. The family lives in military housing and had planned to stay in the community, as Ryan was seeking to retire from the army and obtain a Civilian job, while Jennifer wanted to return to the work force in the real estate industry. Jennifer, Dahlia, and Amy understandably experienced intense grief and continue to struggle with how close Ryan was to retiring when the tragedy occurred. Amy also questions why her dad had to be the one who died, but feels guilty when she thinks about this because she doesn't want to wish tragedy on others. Jennifer and the girls are receiving ongoing traumatic grief counseling and family therapy that focuses on military losses. Directly following the event, the family received outside therapy. Dahlia received trauma-focused CBT (Cohen, Mannarino, & Cozza, 2014) delivered in a modified format at school through a focus on visuals, storytelling, and adaptations due to her age. Amy received Trauma and Grief Component Therapy for Adolescents (TGCTA) (Saltzman et al., 2017). In addition, given that military students are enrolled in both schools, the school psychologist had let the school community, specifically the teachers, know that he is available for counseling, and monitors miltary youth for secondary trauma on an ongoing basis. He runs a support group for military youth, co-led by a social worker, in both school buildings and pays particular attention to miltary youth and family members who have impending or current deployments. He also sends fact sheets to teachers about traumatic grief (Trauma-Focused Cognitive Behavioral Therapy National Therapist Certification Program TF-CBT, 2020), and is particularly mindful of needed mental health supports now that the 1-year anniversary of Ryan's death is near.

Coupled with the grief and trauma associated with the anniversary of the death and the stressors of now being a single parent, Jennifer is also struggling with important decisions, such as being required to leave the military base with her family. Dahlia and Amy are also understandably grieving. Amy feels some specific guilt because her last interaction with her dad, through Skype, was a negative one, arguing with him about keeping up with her homework as an eighth-grade student, which adds to the complicated grief and trauma she experiences. She has benefited from the (TGCTA) (Saltzman et al., 2017) as well as the ongoing counseling and support received within the school and from her outside therapist. Dahlia, the younger sibling, tends to agree with Amy and her perceptions of situations. In this case, she has some anger toward her sister and her mom for not trying to convince her dad to retire sooner, and feels that this tragedy could have been avoided, thus adding to her grief and loss. Jennifer is increasingly losing her temper with her daughters in typical situations, such as failing to follow through on chores. Jennifer is also uncertain about what work she will pursue and needs assistance in filing paperwork to ensure that the family's military benefits are maintained and continued over time. Ryan's parents have moved closer to the family and have tried to assist with the paperwork and running the household, which has been a source of comfort; Jennifer's parents are deceased. The family has many friends in the community since they have resided there for 5 years. However, the area is rather expensive to live in. Although Jennifer would like to stay and keep the girls in the same schools and in a stable environment, she is unsure how she can continue to afford living there.

In addition to the mental health counseling supports delivered at school for both girls and the coordination and collaboration with the community therapist (with Jennifer's consent and Amy's asssent) and the ongoing monitoring of the needed mental health services, the school psychologist and school social worker have also helped Jennifer with finding after-school care and have delivered ADAPT (Gewirtz et al., 2009) in a modified format and with the involvement of the paternal grandparents, who are also experiencing trauma and grief due to the loss of their son. The school psychologist has also helped the grandparents to obtain outside therapy while in town. To coordinate and facilitate all of these efforts, a wraparound team has been created, and involves key members who address major life domains, such as housing and recreation (Bruns et al., 2004). The key members are Jennifer, Amy, Dahlia, the paternal grandparents, and a close family friend who is also connected to the military. In addition to the range of mental health inteventions and supports just described, the primary wraparound goals and proposed solutions as identifed by the family are as follows:

- The wraparound team sets a goal, based on family priorites, to prioritize community-based employment for Jennifer and housing for the entire family within the community so the girls can remain in the school district and stay connected to their community (Bruns et al., 2004). Activities to meet these goals involve helping Jennifer contact a local agency that facilitates affordable housing and reach out to community members to help her with her real estate license renewal and building her professional network. In particular, Jennifer envisons a niche area of assisting retired military service members to find housing and transitioning out of the military.

- The team should ensure that Jennifer and the paternal grandparents have access to parenting supports and family therapy, in which boundaries in parenting and limit setting can be negotiated, particularly as the girls reach the adolescent years. Further, members can engage in continued assessments about the need for ongoing supports, such as trauma-focused CBT, which includes relaxation techniques for caregivers (Cohen & Mannarino, 2011) or other mental health interventions, based on how the family responds to what is already being provided. They can also continue to monitor any new needs for mental health services based on the family decisions that are being made while experiencing continued stress, trauma, and grief.

- The team should consider using funds and supports to offer a bereavement summer camp experience specifically for military-connected youth (Tragedy Assistance Program for Survivors, n.d.).

- The team should review data that are already being collected to ensure that the girls have access to at least one person in their school with whom they can discuss a problem to maintain positive social relationships (Lucier-Greer et al., 2015; Lucier-Greer et al., 2016). In addition, ongoing academic screening and school climate data, already being collected as part of the Tier 1 intervention, should be monitored to check on how the girls are doing and to adjust behavioral, academic, and mental health/social–emotional interventions as needed (Stoiber, 2014). The team can determine if there is a need for more specialized data collection with the girls in the mental health area, related to trauma, grief, depression, and anxiety concerns. As part of current mental health interventions, coordination is occurring already with the outside therapists.

- The team should help the girls and their mother to address, from their perspective, how to respond to others in the community and the school when discussing the tragedy. They should talk with them about their wishes for honoring their fallen service member and about describing their wishes with others. Community members may have well-intentioned ideas about honoring Ryan, but these ideas may not be aligned with the desires of the family and their cultural and personal preferences. The school psychologist can serve as a conduit in collaborating and consulting with teachers and other school personnel (Rosenfield & Humphrey, 2012).

Given that this tragic event requires specialized, sensitive, and individualized family supports within an MTSS framework, intensive wraparound supports, along with the Tier 1/Tier 2 supports offered at school and/or in collaboration with community providers, would be key to a comprehensive, integrated, and sensitive approach to the family during this tragic time. The needs of the family in this scenario were satisfied through individual counseling and mental health services related to traumatic grief, and through applying a trauma-focused lens to the work.

CONCLUSION

School psychologists can play an active and integral role in addressing the mental health needs of military youth and their families and preventing adverse outcomes by implementing MTSS. Further, they should give particular attention to military families who are facing a deployment. This chapter reviewed the pertinent military literature that can be applied to an MTSS model for addressing the wellness and mental health concerns for military families. This chapter particularly focused on the military deployment literature and how school psychologists can apply it when supporting military families, in line with their obligation to support their mental health needs. Given the significant number of military youth and their families who are impacted by their service and sacrifice, both in their daily life and at school, our institutions, including our schools, are called upon to wrap our best skills, hearts, and minds around this wonderful population, who have given so much to our country and, in some sad cases, have given their lives.

CHAPTER 6

Support during School Transitions

with Gina Coffee

Consider the Parker family. They are currently living in Speicher, Germany, a village outside of Spangdahlem Air Base, the Air Force base where Mr. Parker is stationed and Mrs. Parker works full time as a general-schedule government employee. The Parkers have a daughter, Kate, who is in the second grade at Spangdahlem Elementary School, which she has attended since kindergarten. She has many friends in her class and in their neighborhood; enjoys school and loves her second-grade teacher; spends much of her time at the school library, as she has become a voracious reader of chapter books; and was invited to join an enrichment program this school year. Mr. Parker recently received orders for an assignment at Ramstein Air Base, approximately 72 miles away, so the family will be relocating to Ramstein, Germany, at the end of the school year. As the Parkers begin planning for the move, the focus of many of their conversations has been Kate's transition to a new town and school as she begins the third grade.

Kate's move to another base is not unusual, as military-connected children typically make an average of nine transitions during their educational careers (Sanchez, 2012; as cited in Fenning et al., 2013). Given that transitions are very common and involve a new educational setting each time, there are special considerations that may require unique and special attention from school personnel. In Chapter 4, the impact of transitions and military moves on students' social development was covered; Chapter 5 explored the impact of relocation and deployment on students' mental health; and Chapter 7, on legislation pertaining to educational needs, provides a detailed analysis of the Military Interstate Compact (Military Interstate Children's Compact Commission, 2015). In this chapter, we continue to examine

---

Gina Coffee, PhD, NCSP, is a school psychologist practicing in the Denver Public Schools.

the impact of relocation by studying transitions within the context of students' academic progress. The chapter concludes with a discussion of ways to promote academic success during transitions and relocations, including recommendations for school psychologists to consider as they support military-connected students, their families, and school personnel.

Before exploring the impact of relocations on military-connected students' educational progress, let's review the demographic data regarding the distribution of military-connected children in schools. As stated in Chapter 1, within the active-duty force, most children fall within the preschool (0–5 years) and primary school (6–14 years) age groups (Clever & Segal, 2013). In particular, approximately 42% of dependent children of active-duty families are preschool age, and about the same percentage are primary school age (Clever & Segal, 2013). In contrast, approximately 16% of dependent children of active-duty families are high school age or older (Clever & Segal, 2013). Within the National Guard and Reserves families, children tend to be older, with most military-connected youth being of primary school age, and the remaining children relatively equally distributed between preschool and high school age or older (Clever & Segal, 2013). As described elsewhere in this book, despite the large population of young children in military families, there is a paucity of literature covering early childhood education in the military (Clever & Segal, 2013). We certainly acknowledge the need for access to early childhood services and high-quality preschool environments, although early childhood education is outside the scope of this book. As such, we urge those who work with young military-connected children to consult with the Educational and Developmental Intervention Services (EDIS) available on military installations.

Second, in addition to knowing the age distribution of military-connected youth, it is helpful to revisit the settings in which they are generally educated, before beginning to examine the impact of school transitions. As described extensively in Chapter 2, children in military families usually attend DoDEA or non-DoDEA (or Civilian) schools. There are advantages in attending DoDEA schools, as "DoDEA schools are regarded as models of excellence" (Masten, 2013a, p. 202). For example, data indicate that students who attend DoDEA schools perform well on standardized tests of achievement. Further, Black and Latinx students who attend DoDEA schools perform better on the National Assessment of Educational Progress (NAEP) than those who attend public schools (Smrekar, Guthrie, Owens, & Sims, 2001), and the achievement gap in DoDEA schools is narrower (DoDEA, 2015; Smrekar et al., 2001). Finally, DoDEA schools have established system-wide policies and procedures (e.g., graduation requirements), making transitions between schools less cumbersome and worrisome. However, in 2011, only approximately 86,000 students were enrolled in DoDEA schools, and 4% were not children of military families (Clever & Segal, 2013). This means that the number of students enrolled in DoDEA schools in 2011 represented less than 13% of school-age military-connected youth, and most of these youth attended Civilian schools (Clever & Segal, 2013).

Within this context, consider that on average, military-connected youth will move with their active-duty families approximately every 2 to 3 years (Clever & Segal, 2013). Given that military families are stationed in the continental United States (82%); Hawaii, Alaska, and U.S. territories (5%); Europe (5%); East Asia and Pacific regions (4%); and North

Africa, Sub-Saharan Africa, and Central and South America (less than 1%), it is conceivable that military-connected children will relocate nationally or internationally, and between DoDEA schools and Civilian schools.

With these variables in mind, it becomes even more important for us to critically explore the impact of relocation. In moving forward with this discussion, we want to reiterate that, as in previous chapters, the experiences of military-connected youth ought to be studied and understood through a lens of resiliency (e.g., Masten, 2013b; Milburn & Lightfoot, 2013; Palmer, 2008; Russo & Fallon, 2015). As such, we do not assume that children of military families are at a disadvantage due to frequent moves and transitions between schools. In fact, Weber and Weber (2005) found that parents' attitudes toward moving improve as the number of moves increases, and this change of attitude promotes adolescents' resilience. Similarly, "third-culture kids" who travel internationally experience certain advantages that can also promote resilience (Jordan, 2002). Finally, transitioning between schools may also provide military-connected youth with opportunities to improve their educational progress (Marchant & Medway, 1987). We take the position that although transitioning among schools presents certain challenges for youth in military families, we can work together as educators and communities to ease the challenges and illuminate the resiliency and many strengths that military families have.

MILITARY FAMILIES' EXPERIENCES TRANSITIONING BETWEEN SCHOOLS

Given the comprehensive nature of content knowledge and skills that students acquire from elementary school through high school, one can imagine the impact that relocations have at any point in a student's life. The frequent and unpredictable relocations that military youth experience may require greater adjustments for their academic success. For example, through focus groups conducted with military-connected students ($n = 39$), parents ($n = 24$), and school staff ($n = 35$), Bradshaw et al. (2010) identified several themes associated with school transitions. Although many themes were related to disruptions in social networks and supports, participants also reported stress associated with academic challenges, such as concerns about the quality of education, differences in school requirements, supports for students with special needs, a misalignment of curriculum resulting in students either repeating content or missing critical content altogether, completing graduate requirements in a timely manner, and logistical issues, such as transfer of records.

THE MILITARY INTERSTATE CHILDREN'S COMPACT

Unfortunately, in the lives of military families, these concerns are neither new nor unique to the participants in the studies. Citing Esqueda, Astor, and De Pedro (2012), Masten stresses "the Department of Defense, the MCEC, the Obama administration, and the Department of Education worked together to reduce such barriers and provide resources to support the academic achievement of military children throughout the country" (Masten, 2013a, p. 202). One such support is the Interstate Compact on Educational Opportunity for Military Children, commonly referred to as "the Compact" (ICEOMC; Military Interstate Children's Compact Commission, 2015). Taking into account the significant barriers that students in military families can encounter during school transitions, the Compact was designed to facilitate the provision of supports specifically for youth who are transitioning to public schools in the United States and its territories. The legislative components of the Compact and a more detailed analysis of the commitments of the sending and receiving schools are provided in Chapter 7. Given the Compact's important role in supporting academic transitions among military youth, however, the key components are outlined as follows:

> [Facilitate] the timely enrollment of children [from] military families and [ensure] that they are not placed at a disadvantage due to the difficulty in the transfer of education records from the previous school district(s) or variations in entrance/age requirements.
>
> [Facilitate] the student placement process through which children of military families are not disadvantaged by variations in attendance requirements, scheduling, sequencing, grading, course content, or assessment.
>
> [Facilitate] the qualification and eligibility for enrollment, educational programs and participation in extracurricular academic, athletic, and social activities.
>
> [Facilitate] the on-time graduation of children of military families.
>
> [Provide] for the promulgation and enforcement of administrative rules implementing the provisions of [the] Compact.
>
> [Provide] for the uniform collection and sharing of information between and among member states, schools, and military families under [the] Compact.
>
> [Promote] coordination between this compact and other compacts affecting military children.
>
> [Promote] flexibility and coordination between the educational system, parents, and the student in order to achieve educational success for the student (Council of State Governments, 2008, pp. 1–2 as cited in Esqueda, Astor, & De Pedro, 2012, p. 67).

SPECIAL CONSIDERATIONS IN TRANSITIONS OF MILITARY YOUTH WITH DISABILITIES

Military youth with disabilities may require special attention by school psychologists, because they may be at particular risk of not experiencing a continuity of academic supports, including changes in special education services as they transition from one school to another. Recognizing this risk, Jagger and Lederer (2014) conducted a study specifically examining the impact of geographic mobility on military children's access to special education services. Specifically, they collaborated with the National Council on Disability (NCD) and one particular branch of the military to identify participants from three installations (each in a separate state) to engage in focus groups and individual interviews. Participants included adult caregivers of individuals with disabilities (*n* = 39) and military and community service providers (*n* = 62). All adult caregivers were enrolled in the DoD Exceptional Family Member Program (EFMP), and the service providers were generally from EFMP, the School Liaison Program, DoD schools, and EDIS. Through 27 focus groups and 10 individual interviews, Jagger and Lederer (2014) identified the challenges, the military-specific resources, and the recommendations involved with transitioning military-connected youth with disabilities and their families.

Jagger and Lederer (2014, p. 18) note the primary challenges that military families and their children with disabilities face, as follows (in order from most to least frequent):

Parents feel they must battle school systems.

Different state/local educational authorities' approaches to achieving educational goals lead to parental concerns about quality of services.

Uncertainty about place of residence limits proactive planning and precludes warm handoff.

[Receiving] schools are not prepared for student arrival when records were sent in advance.

Americans with Disabilities Act of 1990 non-compliance or inaccessibility.

In particular, parents noted that they encounter differences in processes for determining eligibility and educational services (e.g., access to applied behavior analysis supports for children with autism spectrum disorder [ASD]) and, as a consequence, are unsure of the appropriateness or quality of services their children will receive at the new school. Parents also reported strained relationships with schools when they encountered obstacles, such as physically inaccessible schools, or a perceived a lack of supports. Some parents perceived that schools delayed the provision of special education services, knowing that families would soon move again. Relatedly, participants noted that although they preferred to begin planning early, early planning was not always possible if families did not have specific information about where they would live. This challenge becomes particularly difficult when certain resources (e.g., enrollment in DoD schools or EDIS) are only available at certain installations and not to all residents at the installations.

Participants in their study also identified the following resources (in order from most to least frequent) to support military families who have children with disabilities (Jagger & Lederer, 2014, p. 20):

EFMP [Military One Source, n.d]

School liaisons

Directors of special education at [receiving] schools, as an information source

Staff at [sending] schools that proactively assist with transferring records

Advocacy programs like Specialized Training of Military Parents (STOMP), Task.mil, and other local and state resources

The Exceptional Family Member Program

Jagger and Lederer's (2014) findings highlight the outstanding resources provided through the EFMP, which military families can be referred to by school psychologists (Military One Source, 2020b). Military families who suspect that they have a child with special education needs or have a child with already identified needs benefit from being knowledgeable about and having access to the EFMP, which provides substantial advocacy and support. Military-connected youth with special educational requirements are supported in a number of ways. First of all, through this program, the documented needs of the family, including special education needs of military students, are considered as part of the military assignment given to a military parent, although it is understood that the military mission remains the primary consideration. For military families living on installations, Family Support Providers help with connecting them to available military and community resources, as well as with applying for necessary supports (Military One Source, 2020b). In addition, Special Needs Consultants are available to help military families in accessing special education and health supports. These consultations include supporting military families by staying on a call when they access and navigate complex health and educational resources. Finally, there are outstanding online resources for military families of children with special education needs that are available and accessible on the Military One Source website (Military One Source, 2020b). See Table 6.1 for a summary of the resources that support the academic transitions of military youth with suspected and/or documented disabilities. School psychologists can share and review these resources with families, particularly as they transition from a school in one state to a school in another, or, in some cases, relocate to a school overseas.

Special Considerations for Youth with ASD

School transitions may be particularly difficult for military youth with ASD, and school psychologists should be particularly mindful of how to support military families with one or more children who have ASD during relocations and school changes. Davis and Finke (2015) conducted a study that incorporated the relocation and separation experiences of military families who have children with ASD. Based on semistructured qualitative interviews they conducted with 15 parents and/or caregivers of children with ASD, Davis and Finke (2015) categorized barriers, supports, and/or negative impacts participants experienced as a result of relocations. The authors' analysis resulted in numerous defined themes. Themes identified as barriers and the percentage of participants who noted these barriers included delayed therapeutic service or therapeutic service effectiveness (67%), limited providers or therapeutic services (80%), lack of therapeutic service continuity (67%), lack of therapeutic service quality (67%), starting over (80%), and lack of external support (60%). Themes identified as supports, or aspects of relocation that facilitated engagement in therapeutic services, included therapeutic service quality (67%) and therapeutic service maintenance (60%). Finally, participants identified the negative impacts of relocation: child emotional or behavioral reactions (87%), family stress (53%), and lack of control (53%).

TABLE 6.1. Resources to Support the Academic Transitions of Military Youth with Suspected and/or Documented Disabilities

Name of resource	Brief description
Special Needs Parent Toolkit (DoD Exceptional Family Member Program, 2014)	An online downloadable parent toolkit with six modules with information and resources designed specifically for military families with children with suspected and/or documented disabilities. The modules are as follows: (1) Birth to Age 3; (2) Special Education; (3) TRICARE Health Benefits; (4) Families in Transition; (5) Advocating for Your Child, and (6) Resources and Support. The Birth to Age 3 module has pertinent information for parents if they suspect their child has a delay and explains how early intervention works and how to go about seeking access. A feature of the special education model is a clear explanation of IDEA, due process rights, and information for families with children who have IEPS in navigating moves within and across states. The TRICARE module provides an explanation of how health benefits work for military families, including information about home health care, obtaining counseling, a section on IDEA and health care and how to seek consultation with health care advisors. Highlights of the module on family transitions and moves are practical information about EFMP enrollment and resources and resources for move and transitions, including tips for talking to children about moving, available supports through EFMP, schools and special considerations for moving overseas. In addition, this module contains extensive information about traveling with children, deployment, spousal employment, deployment and preparing for a disaster. Finally, this module contains highly relevant information for parents with adolescents with disabilities that are transitioning to adulthood, such as benefits through social security and Medicaid, legal guardianship, and independent living. The module on advocating for your child covers how to become and stay organized with medical, health and educational records, how to effectively communicate with service providers and how to advocate for the medical/health and educational rights of military children with disabilities. There is also a section on how to support learning as a parent. The module on resources and supports contains information about military-specific, federal, state, and community organizations/agencies which offer support to military families.
Military One Source Education Directory for Children with Special Education Needs (Military One Source, 2020a)	The Military One Source website contains two online searchable directories: one for early intervention (birth to 3) and the second for school-age children (3 to 21) that military families can access in one place to locate special education resources and state special educational guidelines. EFMP support staff can be located by accessing their military installation and searching by zip code. Information about military installations in each respective state can also be obtained.
DoD Directory: Early Intervention, Special Education and Related Services in OCONUS Communities (DoD, 2014)	This is a directory of schools in military communities outside of the Continental United States that contains information about the schools in each military location that can accommodate a range of special education/disability categories. The directory lists the special education categories that can be accommodated in each school, with the caveat that professionals need to make the determination about the supports required and cannot solely rely on knowing that an individual student has been identified with one of the special education eligibility categories.

Davis and Finke's research is illuminating for school psychologists, who are in a unique position to support military youth with ASD as they transition from school to school. The resources provided in Table 6.1 are a starting point in helping military families to connect with military programs, particularly locating and collaborating with their EFMP support staff, as available. When relocating in settings outside of the United States, the Department of Defense Directory of Early Intervention, Special Education and Related Services in OCONUS Communities (DoD, 2014) may be particularly useful, because it provides the names and locations of school sites that are set up to accommodate children with specific disabilities, including ASD. School psychologists can ensure that special education services continue as seamlessly as possible by reminding the sending and receiving schools that these services should be comparable in the new setting and not delayed owing to paperwork or reevaluation issues, consistent with "The Compact" (National Military Family Association, 2020), which should hold true for all children with special education needs, but may be particularly critical for military youth with ASD. An illustration of how school psychologists could accommodate military youth with ASD experiencing relocation is provided in the following case example.

The Wallace family of five live together in a Fort Bragg North Carolina military installation. Ms. Wallace is an officer in the army, and Mr. Wallace is a high school English teacher. Calle is a 4-year-old with a medical diagnosis of ASD who attends an on-base early childhood program. She also receives occupational therapy and speech and language services. The other children are 6-year-old twins, Miley and Jason, who are meeting academic expectations. Miley has some speech articulation concerns and also has an individualized education plan (IEP) for speech. Ms. Wallace has just received orders that she and her family are being transferred to Fort Irwin, California, a military base where she will spend a few months before deploying to an overseas assignment. The family has searched for housing, which will not be on the base, but in a neighboring community that is the catchment school district for the school where Mr. Wallace will be a teacher and the children will be enrolled as students. The school psychologist working on the military base, Mr. James, sets up a meeting with the family and the North Carolina-based EFMP liaison, Ms. Salazar, to support the family in their transition. This meeting also includes the EFMP liaison for the Fort Irwin base, Mr. Irving, who has been identified by accessing the Military One Source Education Directory for Children with Special Education Needs (Military One Source, 2020a) found in Table 6.1. In addition, the special education and general education resources in the public school district to which the family is moving in California are researched. To follow up, Ms. Salazar takes the lead in setting up a subsequent meeting, which will include her, Mr. Irving, Mr. James, and Mr. and Ms. Wallace. At that follow-up meeting, the special education and general education needs of the children are discussed, and the IEPs currently in place are discussed. Then, a third meeting is scheduled with all parties and the school psychologist in the receiving school, Ms. Davis, to introduce the family and provide a time line for the move.

Afterward, Ms. Davis, as the receiving school-based contact, begins to process all IEP paperwork and academic information about the three children. She then works with the family to research early childhood programs in the receiving school district for Calle, and notifies the special education team about the special education supports and services currently being given to both Calle and Miley. Ms. Davis then facilitates special education IEP meetings for both Calle and Miley, in which the existing IEPs and related services in North Carolina are reviewed. For both Calle and Miley, the team accepts the existing IEP, consistent with the Military Interstate Children's Compact provisions. Calle is enrolled in the district's early intervention program and also will continue to receive the same amount of occupational therapy and speech and language services, consistent with the IEP. The social worker on the IEP team and the EFMP receiving liaison, Mr. Irving, also support the family with referrals for respite supports and a referral to a support group for families with members who are about to deploy overseas. The team decides to begin the school year with the existing IEP paperwork and use the academic placement and assessment in North Carolina to determine the best educational program and teacher for Jason. It plans to reconvene in 1 month, once the family has settled in, and to help the family as needed while Ms. Wallace prepares for her deployment, which is scheduled to occur in 3 months. The team also wants to help evaluate how all of the children transition, but particularly Calle, who may face difficulty adjusting to an entirely new home in a different state and school environment. Given that deployment dates change frequently and that the educational programs and supports for the children may need to be adjusted, Ms. Davis agrees to be the point of contact whom the parents can call on if their situation changes or any additional assistance is needed. Further, the California special education team gives the family the names of military parents with children in the early childhood program and in each grade who have agreed to provide resources and support. This case example shows how the entire Wallace family could be assisted, with a particular emphasis on maintaining Calle's existing early childhood interventions and supports without interruption and by ensuring that a "warm handoff" occurs as the family transitions to a new deployment setting.

EXTRACURRICULAR ACTIVITIES

For many youth, another central component of the educational experience is participation in extracurricular activities, and relocation can hinder the extent to which they can participate. In team sports, for example, military families and school staff have reported difficulties with joining teams (especially when a family move occurs after tryouts when teams have already been established), maintaining team composition, and building team cohesion when students are at risk of moving away from or to a different school midseason (Bradshaw et al., 2010). Furthermore, participation in certain extracurricular activities is often reliant on "students' name recognition, history of service in the school, and overall popularity" (Bradshaw et al., 2010, p. 95), perhaps placing students who are new to a school at a disadvantage. In contrast, military-connected youth have found that joining noncompetitive clubs may offer them an opportunity to become involved in their new schools and build social networks (Bradshaw et al., 2010).

School psychologists and other school professionals should be encouraged to meet with military youth as they transition into new school settings. One vital strategy would be to make sure that these youth know which extracurricular clubs and sports are available to them. Learning about their interests and prior activities is an important place to start a conversation with a military youth transitioning into a new school. Then connecting that youth through an intentional introduction with other students who have similar interests and are involved in sports and clubs is another way to make them feel included and welcomed. School psychologists can use their agency to advocate for the relaxation of hard team-tryout deadlines with key personnel, such as coaches and athletic directors, to the degree possible, which is also consistent with what is stated in the Compact. Even if hard deadlines for tryouts have passed and cannot be negotiated, there can be creative ways of involving military youth in extracurricular activities and sports. For example, if a deadline for the tryout for a competitive sports team, such as baseball has passed, then the school psychologist and others can help the military youth to start a recreational baseball club at a local gym, within their military installation, or through a park district. Military youth could also be encouraged to start clubs and activities that are of interest to them.

THE ROLE OF THE SCHOOL PSYCHOLOGIST IN SUPPORTING STUDENTS DURING TRANSITIONS

As we continue to explore the role of the school psychologist in supporting military students during academic transitions, consider the recommendations that follow the case study of the Devine family and contemplate how they might be applied to the family's upcoming move.

Ms. Devine is a single mother of twin boys, Caleb and Joshua, who are in the fifth grade, and she is serving in the army. She is currently stationed at Fort Hood in Texas, an army post centrally located between Killeen and Copperas Cove, and she and her sons live on the post. Ms. Devine has been stationed at Fort Hood for 30 months, and is making plans to retire from military service and return to her hometown of Chicago in July. While living at Fort Hood, Caleb and Joshua have attended an elementary school together on the post, and Caleb has been receiving IEP supports for a specific learning disability in reading comprehension. Ms. Devine feels that Caleb has made tremendous gains since starting school, and she credits his teachers and the school psychologist for ensuring that he receives individualized supports that target his needs.

In preparing to relocate, Ms. Devine has been spending her evenings after the boys go to sleep researching the schools back home and also chatting with her friends and family about options in Chicago. She has also consulted with the school psychologist and the EFMP liaison assigned to her. Given her relocation history with the Army, she knows moving can be academically difficult for children, and she wants to be sure that neither of her sons lose the knowledge and skills they have gained in the latter part of their elementary years. She also knows that transitioning to middle school can be stressful for children under ordinary circumstances, and moving to another school district, much less another city and state, may magnify this stress. Finally, an additional consideration for Ms. Devine is that she wishes to enroll her sons in one of the city's Catholic schools.

As we have seen in the other case illustrations throughout this book, school psychologists—because they are trained to support the academic, behavioral, and social–emotional development of children and adolescents—can be instrumental in coordinating supports for military-connected youth, like Caleb and Joshua, who are transitioning from their current school to a new one. In this case example, school psychologists can be a critical part of a continuum of care in their collaborative and consultative roles as they help the Devines transition to a new setting and ensure that all school personnel, particularly those in private schools, are informed about the tenets of the Compact, and can see to it that the transition of special education and IEP supports for military youth with disabilities occurs seamlessly. The following critical functions of school psychologists involved in supporting the academic transitions of military youth are largely informed by the work of Russo and Fallon (2015) and De Pedro, Esqueda, Cederbaum, and Astor (2014).

CRITICAL FUNCTIONS AND ROLES OF SCHOOL PSYCHOLOGISTS IN SUPPORTING TRANSITIONS

- As a first step in supporting military youth in schools when their families relocate, as has been stressed throughout this book, particularly in Chapter 1, school psychologists should adopt a resiliency model of understanding and supporting military-connected youth during academic transitions. As noted by many (e.g., Masten, 2013b; Milburn & Lightfoot, 2013; Palmer, 2008; Russo & Fallon, 2015), although military youth do experience stressors unique to the military lifestyle, these stressors do not typically translate into negative outcomes for children and adolescents. Rather, these youth are often characterized by resiliency, and researchers who work with military families have used various models of resiliency or stress models to frame their work with this group (e.g., see models cited in Russo & Fallon, 2015). Notably, researchers have found that military youth often become more resilient as the number of moves they experience increases (Weber & Weber, 2005). We recommend that school psychologists study and adopt these models and use them to inform their work with military students who are transitioning away from or to their schools.

- Beyond accessing the resources provided in Table 6.1 and throughout the book, school psychologists who work with a specific military family should consult with other school psychologist colleagues who serve a military population about specific situations that arise. For example, the National Association of School Psychologists (NASP, 2016) has a professional community for school psychologists interested in working with military families in the United States and internationally (NASP Communities: Military Families), and Division 19 of the American Psychological Association (APA) specifically focuses on military psychology (APA Division 19, 2016). In addition to accessing research from professional organizations, school psychologists may also find support from, and engage with, others who are committed to supporting military-connected youth during transitions.

- We also recommend that school psychologists consider the varied contexts in which military youth transitions occur. Military youth are educated in a wide variety of school environments, as described in detail in Chapter 2. The children and adolescents of military families typically attend DoDEA schools or non-DoDEA (or Civilian) schools. Schools within the DoDEA system are attuned to the military lifestyle and the sometimes idiosyncratic needs of students of military families. As such, they are equipped with specific resources and are ready to assist when students transition between schools in the DoDEA system. It behooves school psychologists who work both within and outside of the DoDEA system to learn about the DoDEA system, so they may fully support their students who are transitioning either within DoDEA schools or between DoDEA and non-DoDEA schools. Similarly, we recommend that school psychologists who work within and outside of the DoDEA system become familiar with the non-DoDEA school systems to which their students are transitioning. Also of critical importance is becoming deeply familiar with the Compact, so that it can be used as an advocacy tool by school psychologists who are either helping military youth make an academic transition from or to a school they work in (Military Interstate Children's Compact Commission, 2015). Finally, we recommend that school psychologists at both the sending and receiving schools become familiar with the school liaison office (e.g., Aronson, Caldwell, Perkins, & Pasch, 2011) and EFMP offices to help ease the transition for military youth. See Table 6.1 for specific information about accessing military staff who have been trained to facilitate the academic transitions of military youth.

- As school psychologists become familiar with the research conducted with military families and their children, they also should take note of the school-based interventions that have proven to be successful with military-connected youth. Unfortunately, there is a dearth of evaluation data to assist school psychologists in selecting the appropriate interventions (e.g., Brendel, Maynard, Albright, & Bellomo, 2014; Milburn & Lightfoot, 2013). For example, when Brendel et al. (2014) designed their study to conduct a meta-analysis "to examine the effects of school-based interventions on the well-being of military-connected children" (p. 651), they found that they were unable to conduct the meta-analysis because only one quasi-experimental study met their inclusion criteria. Despite the lack of evaluation data, interventions to support transitioning military-connected youth are available for school psychologists to implement with transitioning students in their schools (information about interventions can be found on the Military Child Education Coalition website (*www.militarychild.org*). Once school psychologists become familiar with the available interventions, they may wish to systematically collect evaluation data after implementing them in their schools.

- Another critical function of school psychologists who work with military youth during academic transitions is becoming knowledgeable about the military and community resources that are applicable and accessible to the families they are serving. As already noted, the school liaison, EFMP, and EDIS offices are useful starting points for learning about the programs provided by the military. However, it should be noted these programs may not be available at every military base or post or to every military family. For example, for military families to access EDIS, they must first live on the military installation, and even then, not all families may be entitled to the services (Jagger & Lederer, 2014; *www.edis.army.mil*). As such, the school psychologist needs to not only know which programs are provided by the military to support students' transitions to new schools, but which ones are available to the individual student, as well as how to access them. To navigate these resources, school psychologists may wish to learn about Military Student Transition Consultants (MSTC) who are based in their geographic region or may be contacted via telecommunication (Military Child Education Coalition, 2012). In addition to the services provided by the military, we recommend that school psychologists expand their already comprehensive familiarity with community resources to learn about the non-military community organizations that either already serve military youth and their families or may be open to expanding their services to them. With a knowledge of this network of supports, they may ultimately better advise families, support military-connected youth in transitioning, and coordinate a continuity of care across service providers.

CONSULTATION AND COLLABORATION LENS

We believe that the primary way in which school psychologists may apply their acquired knowledge to support transitioning military youth is through consultation and collaboration with school professionals, families, and students.

- First, together with administrators, student services professionals, and teachers, we advise school psychologists to identify and get to know the military youth in their schools and their families. For school psychologists who work in DoDEA schools, identifying military youth may be simple (as all or most students will be children or adolescents of military families), but the key to effectively supporting them during relocation to another school will be to get to know them and their needs better (Jagger & Lederer, 2014). As a start, school psychologists may wish to create a database of the approximate dates the current students will be relocating and any unique assistance they may need at that time or in preparation for the move. Relatedly, Jagger and Lederer (2014) recommend incorporating the family's anticipated relocation as a standing item in IEP meetings for military students with disabilities. We also advise that school psychologists at DoDEA schools position themselves to be an integral part of the transition process. Doing so allows them to welcome military youth to the new school, coordinate with the former school, and situate the new student to receive supports while transitioning to the new school. School psychologists who work in non-DoDEA schools or whose schools do not routinely enroll military youth will also want to be involved in receiving new students and assist those who are leaving. Depending on the size of a school's military student population, which may be small, it may be beneficial for the school psychologist to collaborate with administrators to find a way to identify military-connected youth when they transfer to the school and to create a database of the identified students, so that individualized supports may be offered as needed. Strategies and recommendations for identifying which students in schools have military connections as part of MTSS were detailed in Chapter 2, and Form 3.1 at the end of Chapter 3 is a tool that could be adapted for this purpose. As discussed in Chapter 7 (on legal issues), school districts are now required to identify military youth through a mandated military student identifier, a component of the ESSA.

- Once school psychologists know which students in their schools are currently connected to the military and have set up a process for being alerted to incoming military students, we recommend that school psychologists at both the sending and receiving schools facilitate the transfer of academic records for all military students and the transfer of psychoeducational evaluations and IEPs for military students receiving special education services (Jagger & Lederer, 2014), as consistent with the provisions of the Compact. By facilitating the transfer of records, school psychologists make them more readily accessible to those working in the receiving school, which will help them to make better decisions about the necessary educational supports for all military students, but particularly those with special education supports already in place. There are several avenues by which school psychologists may facilitate the transfer of academic records. For instance, some families choose to hand carry and deliver their students' records to the receiving school. In this case, schools may choose to accept the records as is for the time being, and may also seek an official transfer of records from the students' former school. In addition, school psychologists at either the sending or the receiving schools may coordinate with one another to facilitate the transfer. Although the school psychologists may not be the ones who actually send or receive the records, their knowledge of their respective schools, school districts and systems, and processes can facilitate the transfer. Further, school psychologists often have the most expertise in the school about special education laws and supports. If the military-connected student who is transferring has an identified disability, school psychologists should collaborate with the EFMP office(s) if this service is available (*www.militaryonesource.mil/efmp*).

- We recommend that school psychologists work with students and families early in the transition process to inform them about the school's or school district's curriculum and assessments and to make themselves available to students and families who may have questions about the similarities and differences in the systems and how they might affect the military youth's educational progress. Relatedly, we recommend that they learn about the services incoming military youth were receiving at their former school, so that they may begin to discuss with the students and their parents how the receiving school might best meet their needs. Like other components of students' transitions, this is an especially important one because initiating this conversation provides an optimal opportunity to listen to the families' experiences and learn about their child's needs and desires related to the school and to communicate the school's commitment to supporting the family and youth during the relocation process. We want to underscore the importance of school psychologists initiating open and honest conversations with families and their children who have disabilities, because the individualized types of services these students will continue to receive at their new school may be dependent on additional factors, such as data from psychoeducational evaluations and IEPs. As noted earlier, Jagger and Lederer (2014) found that military parents of students with disabilities can feel as though their students are no longer receiving adequate supports when transitioning to their new school and that school professionals seem less invested in supporting their child's needs because they know that military youth may only be at their school for a short time. When the services these youth receive at their new school are different from the services they received at their former school, we suggest that school psychologists describe the differences to families and students and work closely with them to answer their questions, address their concerns, and coordinate additional supports either at the school or within the community to ensure all students' needs are being met. In short, school psychologists should advocate for military families and students as they transition across schools. These conversations may also afford school psychologists the opportunity to inform families, as well as colleagues, about the Compact (Military Interstate Children's Compact Commission, 2015) and help them in understanding its provisions.

- We also believe that school psychologists should work toward raising awareness among school professionals about the military lifestyle and the possible needs of military-connected youth and their families. In concert with the professional development activities school psychologists engage in to raise their own awareness, we believe the education of other professionals can occur on multiple levels. First, with the support of the school and school district administrators, school psychologists can develop and deliver in-service sessions to all interested professionals in their building(s) or school district. Hosting an in-service session available to all not only underscores the importance of learning about the military lifestyle and the ways it can impact military-connected youth and others, but also communicates that these professionals too have a role to play in supporting this special group. It may also be a prime opportunity to educate school professionals about the Compact's provisions (Military Interstate Children's Compact Commission, 2015) regarding transitioning youth, as they navigate entry into extracurricular activities such as sports and clubs. In addition to raising awareness at the universal level, school psychologists should make themselves available to consult with teachers and other school professionals who work directly with military youth to individualize supports that specifically target their needs.

- In connection with raising awareness and consulting with school professionals, we also advise school psychologists and educators to implement and evaluate school-based interventions to support military students' academic needs. As we noted earlier, Brendel et al. (2014) found that although these interventions are implemented in schools, there is still a need for program evaluation showing outcome data that demonstrate the programs' effectiveness. Building upon their professional expertise in working with military youth and their professional training in data-based decision making, consultation, and collaboration, school psychologists can effectively organize schools' efforts around implementing and evaluating interventions to promote academic progress of these students. In particular, we recommend that they first collaborate with student services personnel to establish a multidisciplinary team invested in supporting military students. The team may then choose to conduct a needs assessment to identify the specific needs military youth in their school(s) have during transitions, and once needs have been identified, the team may then select, implement, and evaluate interventions informed by the data. As part of this process, we suggest that school psychologists and teams consult the MCEC website (MCEC, 2015) for descriptions of programs that may be suitable for military youth, as well as the literature supporting these youth (e.g., Bradshaw et al., 2010; De Pedro et al., 2014; Milburn & Lightfoot, 2013). For example, on the MCEC website, school professionals may find information about Student 2 Student (S2S; described in Chapter 4 on healthy social development), a student-centered and student-led program designed to ease relocation transitions for students. These programs and others were summarized in Table 4.1 and could be referenced by school psychologists in planning ways to support the social lives of military youth during academic transitions.

- Finally, in view of their knowledge of military families and local community resources, we recommend that school psychologists consult with military and community organizations and share resources with military families and their children, as well as continuing to check for updated and new resources. First, they may wish to consult online military resources, including the contacts available on military-related websites. Some examples of military websites that provide specific supports for military youth and their families during academic transitions are as follows:
    - Military Child Education Coalition: *www.militarychild.org*
    - Military Impacted Schools Association: *http://militaryimpactedschoolsassociation.org*
    - Military One Source: *www.militaryonesource.mil*
    - Student Online Achievement Resources (SOAR): *http://militaryimpactedschoolsassociation.org/soar*
    - DoDEA: *www.dodea.edu*

Aronson et al. (2011), Clever and Segal (2013), Davis and Finke (2015), De Pedro et al. (2014), Jagger and Lederer (2014), and Russo and Fallon (2015) offer additional programs that school psychologists may find helpful when consulting with military families and community organizations.

To sum up, we believe the recommendations we have offered provide a framework for school psychologists who wish to support the academic transitions of military youth and their families depicted in the three case studies presented in the chapter, and other families facing academic transitions as part of military relocations. Through continuing professional development and by using the resources found here and elsewhere, we hope that school psychologists can sharpen their competencies in serving transitioning military youth and their parents, who may just need a little support when they are giving so much to us individually and collectively.

CONCLUSION

The school transitions military youth and families face require careful attention and consideration from school psychologists, other school professionals, and community advocates. Our goal in this chapter is to illuminate the academic context within which relocations occur for military-connected youth and the reported challenges that military families and their children experience during academic transitions. Although the frequency and unpredictability of relocations within the military can present unique situations, we hold the belief that military families and their children often show resiliency in response to such challenges and can be further supported by policies such as the Compact; the local efforts of school psychologists; and collaboration between military-connected youth, families, schools, community organizations, and policy makers.

CHAPTER 7

Legal Aspects of School Supports for Military Youth

This chapter delves into pertinent legislation that applies to the school-related needs of youth connected with the military. It reviews relevant federal legislation and regulations, such as the Department of Defense (DoD) Provision of Early Intervention and Special Education Services to Eligible DoD Dependents (U.S. Department of Defense, 2015), which applies to youth within DoD-administered schools (Schuchs-Gopaul, n.d.); and the Individuals with Disabilities Education Act (IDEA, 2004), which contains educational mandates for serving military-connected youth with disabilities who attend Civilian public schools. The specific provisions within Section 504 of the Rehabilitation Act of 1973 and Title II of the Americans with Disabilities Act (ADA, 1990) that serve military youth are described. The related U.S. Department of Education (DoE) federal guidelines intended to direct school efforts to better support the educational needs of highly mobile youth, including military youth (U.S. Department of Education, 2013), are highlighted. The ESSA, which established new mandates for tracking the academic achievement of military youth, is reviewed (National Military Family Association, 2020). Legislation with applications for military families, including youth with special education needs and medical issues, such as the National Defense Authorization Act (2015), is discussed. The major tenets of the Military Interstate Children's Compact Commission (Council of State Governments, 2013), an agreement adopted by all 50 states and the District of Columbia to support the transition and unique needs of military youth, are also covered. The chapter concludes with case studies that illustrate the applications of these legislative mandates and federal and state guidelines to hypothetical military families.

EVERY STUDENT SUCCEEDS ACT

Accountability and Data Requirements

With a stroke of a pen on December 10, 2015, President Barack Obama signed the ESSA, a reauthorization of the Elementary and Secondary Education Act, into law. The legislation has several provisions of relevance to all students and schools who educate them. Under ESSA, although annual reading and math assessments are required in elementary and middle school grades and once in high school, along with three required science assessments occurring between grades 3 and 12 (Council for Exceptional Children, 2015), significant federal control under the DoE has been turned over to the states. For example, local school districts select the content of the assessments, ensure accountability, and establish priorities for school improvement (Council for Exceptional Children, 2015; Vaillancourt Strobach, 2015). In Illinois, ESSA indicators include chronic absenteeism and standard academic measures. A school climate measure, the 5 Essentials Survey, is also a required indicator. This survey is completed by parents, teachers, students, and administrators as one way of capturing their input (Illinois State Board of Education, 2019a). Measures that assess student growth instead of summative measures focusing solely on proficiency are acceptable under ESSA (Kowalski, 2015), a requirement that aligns with implementing MTSS and is valuable to school psychologists leading MTSS teams. Further, under the ESSA provisions, college enrollment data are now required as part of the state report card (Kowalski, 2015). It may be too early to tell, but one possible implication of ESSA requirements that offer more flexibility to states in selecting assessments is that military youth will be exposed to a wider variety of assessments than in the past compared to their non-military peers who do not move as frequently (National Military Family Association, 2020). School psychologists, as assessment experts, play an important role in helping school teams, military families, and students to understand these different tools and how they could result in different outcomes and interpretations.

Disaggregated-Subgroup Military Data

As in the previous reiteration of the law (the No Child Left Behind Act [NCLB], 2001), accountability data must be disaggregated by race and/or ethnicity and special education status (Splitek, 2016). Under the new data provisions of the ESSA, federal support is provided to states to more accurately define subgroups, including youth connected with the military, youth with racial or ethnic identifications of Asian or Pacific Islander, and youth who are homeless (Council for Exceptional Children, 2015; Kowalski, 2015). The data tracker for military youth is a welcome addition to the ESSA provisions among organizations devoted to advocating for the success of military youth, such as the National Military Family Association (2020) and the Military Child Education Coalition (Splitek, 2016). The ESSA (2015) requires school districts to report the following information about military-connected students to their state education agency:

ESSA requires all states to collect-and-report assessment data on military-connected students, defined to include students with a parent who is a member of the Army, Navy, Air Force, Marine Corps, and Coast Guard on active duty, including full-time National Guard duty (ESSA, 2015, as cited in Mesecar & Soifer, 2018, p. 1).

School psychologists now have a golden opportunity to take a leadership role in using ESSA data effectively to track the progress of important subgroups, particularly racial and/or ethnic minorities, English learners, and military youth. Given that this ESSA requirement is in the first few years of implementation, there is significant variability among the states as to the degree to which the data have been integrated into statewide databases (Mesecar & Soifer, 2018). In addition, the full potential of analyzing and using the military-identifier ESSA data to determine points of intervention to better support military students has not come to fruition. School psychologists, who have expertise in analyzing data and in leading schoolwide teams to effectively use data to support students, can be integral to changing the required collection of data under the ESSA from a mere reporting function to one that has practical utility. Specifically, they can organize these data in a disaggregated and aggregated manner in a user-friendly way for their MTSS teams and for military families, providing an invaluable service.

According to the National Military Family Association (2020), the ESSA requirements apply to the children of active-duty service members, but not to the children of National Guard and Reserve members, and further clarification and policy guidance is needed from the DoE. School psychologists and other school-based mental health professionals can use the ESSA requirement as an opportunity to monitor the academic performance of all identified subgroups, including military youth, in implementing the universal screening and systematic data collection recommendations made in Chapter 3. As described in other parts of the book, Gilreath et al. (2014) offer military-specific modules that can be used to meet the new ESSA requirements. These modules are currently being implemented throughout the California school system and provide a mechanism by which school climate data can be collected for youth in the aggregate and disaggregated for military youth. The California example is an excellent one and shows how a state can address the ESSA requirement that school districts have at least one measure of school quality, such as school climate and safety, as part of their accountability data (Vaillancourt Strobach, 2015). School psychologists should be at the forefront of providing guidance to states about their ESSA accountability measures. Given that the ESSA data collection requirements are fairly new, school psychologists, as data-measurement experts and child advocates, should continue to provide feedback as implementation continues to roll out.

Specialized Instructional Support Personnel Defined

The ESSA provides significant opportunities for school-based mental health professionals, inclusive of school psychologists, to have an integral role in holding schools accountable and in delivering supports for all students, with unique opportunities to serve military youth in a way that has not occurred to date. School psychologists are explicitly defined in the ESSA as school-based mental health service providers. The ESSA also specifically refers to school psychologists as specialized instructional support personnel (SISP) and requires that states consult with SISP in their efforts to support school districts in achieving school success and supporting student outcomes (Vaillancourt Strobach, 2015). This is an outstanding opportunity to increase the visibility of school psychologists and make our role even more essential than it already is.

Moreover, the ESSA allows for Title I funds to be used for the implementation of MTSS, including SWPBS (Vaillancourt Strobach, 2015), which is a model described in this book as a universal/Tier 1 behavioral intervention that can support all students in a school, including military youth. Training and expertise in SWPBS are in the repertoire of many practicing school psychologists. Given the relatively recent authorization of the ESSA, what implementation will look like in future years is yet to unfold. The legislation comes at a critical time for supporting military youth in their academic and school-related success. School psychologists and other school-based mental health professionals, defined as specialized instructional support staff, are well positioned to take the lead in helping states, who now have more autonomy than in the past, to implement the ESSA. School psychologists can work with their local school district and on a state and national level to develop policies and improve technical assistance related to ESSA implementation, particularly in making meaningful use of the military student identifier. Overall, states are at various points in effectively utilizing the ESSA-mandated military-student identifier data to its highest potential. As described by Splitek (2016), writing on behalf of the Military Child Education, an organization that has long advocated for reliable and inclusive data collection with military students in public schools, mandated data collection will only be valuable if the data are analyzed to better serve military students. In short, ESSA data collection needs to move beyond a mere state reporting function to one that is more formative in nature and that can help direct and evaluate system-wide supports for military youth and all students within an MTSS structure. School psychologists can spearhead meaningful data collection efforts at the local level to build on the advocacy of military families and their allies to include a military student identifier within the ESSA (2015) provisions.

Impact Aid

Through the ESSA funding provisions, local school districts that are disadvantaged by military-related tax-exempt property within their school district boundaries (e.g., military bases) qualify for funding (Workforce Democrats Reauthorization of the Elementary and Secondary Education Act, 2015). The major provisions of the previous authorization were retained, including reimbursement to school districts that lose tax revenue for military-related operations in their community (Workforce Democrats Reauthorization of the Elementary and Secondary Act, 2015). The current ESSA authorized provisions feature a "hold harmless" clause, which protects school districts from an abrupt funding drop in situations such as military housing closures, deployments, or unanticipated redistricting or other local decisions that may alter student enrollment (Workforce Democrats Reauthorization of the Elementary and Secondary Education Act, 2015). In addition, the new ESSA regulations align with the newest versions of the National Defense Authorization Act, also recently appropriated in 2016 (National Defense Authorization Act for Fiscal Year 2016, 2015). It is important for school psychologists to be aware of the parameters of impact aid when consulting with their school and district administrators and school attorneys.

Special Education Legislation and Provisions

The needs of military youth in special education are regulated differently, depending on whether the student is enrolled in a DoD-administered or local public school system (Morin, n.d.; Wright & Wright, 2015). (Refer to the extensive information in Chapter 2 about the different school environments in which military youth are educated, including DoD and Civilian public schools.) Special education regulations, which were revised by the DoD and became effective on July 27, 2015, are applicable to military-connected youth in special education who attend DoD-administered schools (Wright & Wright, 2015). As stated throughout the book, most military youth attend local Civilian public school districts (Schuchs-Gopaul, n.d.), which are administered through the DoE under the Individuals with Disabilities Education Act (IDEA, 2004). The major tenets of IDEA (2004) are most likely familiar to school psychologists, who contribute to the completion of comprehensive special education case study evaluations and the development and delivery of IEPs. This section focuses on the major tenets of the recently adopted DoD special education guidelines as well as the DoE guidelines for public school districts that address the specific needs of military-connected students in special education, particularly their high mobility rates.

DoD-Specific Special Education Regulations

The recently released DoD regulations "Provision of Early Intervention and Special Education Services to Eligible DoD Dependents, Final Rule (U.S. Department of Defense, 2015), which pertain to all students in special education attending DoD-administered schools within the United States and internationally, contain several new tenets, which Wright and Wright (2015) state are an improvement over earlier versions in meeting the educational needs of youth with IEPs. One of the major improvements resulting from the new regulations is an option for military parents of youth in DoD schools to file an administrative complaint with the DoD, just as a parent of a student attending a Civilian school would file a special education dispute with a state education agency. In its application, the 2015 regulations made explicit that military youth with disabilities who transfer from Civilian public schools to DoD schools have a right to IEPs equivalent to those in place at previous schools (Wright & Wright, 2015). Wright and Wright (2015) describe an excellent process for highlighting the content of the regulations so that they are easier to follow, which is helpful information for school psychologists both in DoD and in Civilian schools in their work with military youth and families who may be transferring to or from a DoD school. A detailed analysis of the current regulations is beyond the scope of this chapter, and the reader is directed to the Wrightslaw website (Wright & Wright, 2015) and to the actual Department of Defense regulations in the Federal Register (U.S. Department of Defense, 2015), which are also accessible on the Wrightslaw website. Both the Wrightslaw website and a link to the regulations are found in Appendix 7.1. Overall, the U.S. Department of Defense (2015) early intervention and special education regulations are very similar to the IDEA (2004) regulations implemented in Civilian public schools. There are some nuances that are specific to the Department of Defense (DoD) regulations and DoD schools administered by the DoD, rather than in Civilian public schools under the auspices of the Department of Education (DoE). The DoD regulations have specifications that are very similar to the due process rights afforded to children suspected of or having a disability covered under the IDEA (2004), such as active child find procedures, parental or guardian consent procedures, a continuum of placements within the least restrictive environment, and access to the general education curricula to the degree applicable, timely evaluations and IEP procedures, functional behavior assessment procedures, an individual family service plan for infants or toddlers with a disability, access to a multidisciplinary team and evaluation procedures using reliable and multiple measures. Eligibility evaluations cannot be based on a single measure and must be in the student's native language using technically sound instruments. The 13 special education categories found in IDEA (2004), under which youth between the ages of 3 and 21 can qualify, are the same as those listed in the DoD special education regulations. These due process rights are familiar to school psychologists and other school-based mental health providers, so will not be reviewed in detail here. Let's turn next to another important legal act with significant implications for military-connected youth: the National Defense Authorization Act (2015).

NATIONAL DEFENSE AUTHORIZATION ACT

On October 28, 2009, an earlier version of the National Defense Authorization Act (Section 503) established a DoD office specifically for military families with special needs and the Exceptional Family Member Program (EFMP) (U.S. Department of Defense National Defense Authorization Act, 2009). The major components of The EFMP and the downloadable Exceptional Family Member Program Quick Reference Guide (Military One Source, 2020a) are described on the Military One Source website. The links to access these resources are in Appendix 7.1. As described by the DoD (DoD ERMP, n.d.), the EMFP is designed specifically for military families with children who have special health and education needs. The stated purpose of the EMFP is twofold: (1) to consider a family's needs for specialized supports, including the need for special education and/or early intervention services, in military assignments, and (2) to provide a range of supports for families that include help in accessing local resources and assisting families in accessing and determining eligibility for services. As described on the Military One Source website (2020b), each military branch (e.g., Army, Navy, Marine Corps, and Marines) has its own website with resources to assist military personnel who have a family member with special medical and educational needs that can be supported through the EMFP program. On the Military One Source website (2020b), a link is provided to a military installation website where one can enroll in the EFMP program and search for services that are available at a specific military installation. Another important resource for families of individuals with special needs is the *Exceptional Advocate Newsletter Archives,* an electronic newsletter published several times a year with content specific to military families with special needs members (Military One Source, 2018b). The link to access this resource is in Appendix 7.1.

MILITARY INTERSTATE CHILDREN'S COMPACT

So far, we have summarized the major legislation that applies to the educational needs of school-age military youth and supporting their families or guardians during frequent military moves and school transitions. Arguably, the Military Interstate Children's Compact (the Compact) is the most comprehensive landmark legislative reform to date in facilitating educational transitions for military youth (Council of State Governments, 2013). The drafting of the Compact was a joint collaborative effort among the Council of State Governments, the DoD, and key federal, state, and local stakeholders (Military Interstate Children's Compact Commission [MIC3], 2014). As noted, currently all 50 states and the District of Columbia have adopted the Compact and are member states (Council of State Governments, 2013). The Compact has been legislated by each member state, and therefore the Compact language may differ somewhat from the model content language (Council of State Governments, 2013). A map of each state's adopted Compact language is available at the Military Interstate Children's Compact Commission (Council of State Governments, 2013). The link to access the Compact language adopted by each state is in Appendix 7.1. Students covered by the Compact are defined as follows:

> A student enrolled in K–12 in the household of a full-time duty status in the active uniformed services of the United States, including members of the National Guard and Reserves on active duty orders pursuant to 10 USC section 1209 and 1211. (Military Interstate Children's Compact Commission, 2014, p. 3)

The Compact also applies to military members or retired military service personnel who have been severely injured, medically discharged or retired, who have lost their lives during active duty or as a result of injuries sustained while on active duty in each of these categories for up to 1 year (Military Interstate Children's Compact Commission, 2014). In the Compact, the sending school district is the one the student is leaving, and the receiving school district is the new school the student is transferring to. Given that each state educational agency administers eligibility and educational requirements somewhat differently, including culminating graduation requirements, the Compact is focused on easing issues of grade placement, eligibility, programming, and graduation that are often faced by transitioning military youth.

Fenning and colleagues (2013) summarize the following five major provisions of the Compact that member states and, in turn, school districts in those states agree to comply with as part of the agreement: (1) enrollment, (2) course/program placement, (3) attendance, (4) eligibility, and (5) graduation accommodations. Schuchs-Gopaul (n.d.) summarizes additional specific provisions in the Contract pertaining to Section 504 of the Rehabilitation Act and Title II of the ADA (article 10). A receiving school must make reasonable accommodations or modifications for children with an existing 504 plan and in compliance with Title II of the ADA. The specific pertinent model language in the Compact document (Military Interstate Children's Compact Commission, n.d.) is as follows:

> In compliance with the requirements of Section 504 of the Rehabilitation Act, 29 U.S.C.A. Section 794, and with Title II of the Americans with Disabilities Act, 42 U.S.C.A. Sections 12131-12165, the receiving state shall make reasonable accommodations and modifications to address the needs of incoming students with disabilities, subject to an existing 504 or Title II Plan, to provide the student with equal access to education. (Military Interstate Children's Compact Commission, n.d., p. 11)

A summary of the major provisions of the Compact, as described by Fenning et al. (2013) and Schuchs-Gopaul (n.d.), organized by sending and receiving school district agreements for each of the provisions, is highlighted in Table 7.1. As can be seen in Table 7.1, these major provisions allow flexibility in applying differing educational requirements across states, which may result in unique challenges for military youth.

In order to ensure that the provisions of the legislation are carried out, the Compact provides for a national governing body, the "Interstate Commission," also referred to as the "Military Interstate Children's Compact Commission" (MIC3), a governing body consisting of representatives from each state and the District of Columbia and other key stakeholders as *ex officio* members (Military Interstate Children's Compact Commission, n.d.). The MIC3 oversees the implementation of the Compact, including compliance and training (Military Interstate Children's Compact Commission, n.d.). Each state representative, who is the State Commissioner or a designee, has a vote on actions of the group. The MIC3 serves as a national coordinating body that resolves disputes among states, has a national staff, and is organized through an Executive Committee and four subcommittees (e.g., Rules, Finance, Compliance, and Training) (Military Interstate Children's Compact Commission, n.d.). One of the actions of the Commission was the adoption of rules through which the Compact would operate with "flexibility to make reasonable changes or clarification as the need arises through amendment, advisory opinions, and training opportunities" (Interstate Commission on Educational Opportunity for Military Children Rules, 2012, p. 1). The Commission Rules were originally adopted in November 2009, with the most recent version adopted with amendments on November 16, 2012.

TABLE 7.1. Military Interstate Children's Compact Major Provisions and District Responsibilities

Enrollment	Placement	Attendance	Eligibility	Graduation
• Educational records • Immunization • K–1 enrollment	• Courses • Programs • IEP	Appropriate excused absences	• Enrollment during deployment • Power of attorney • Extracurricular	Accommodations to facilitate on-time graduation
Sending district:				
Equips family with unofficial school records. Sends official transcript to receiving school within 10 days of getting request.		Allows for excused absences to visit with parent or legal guardian during deployment cycle. Schools have flexibility in approving absences during testing for those with excessive absences.	Allows attendance in home school during deployment even if the caregiver does not live in attendance area (caregiver provides transportation). Accepts caregiver power of attorney. Facilitates extracurricular activities even if deadline for tryout missed; doesn't ensure spot.	Works with receiving school in the event that the new school cannot make reasonable accommodations for courses and exit exams—in this case, sending district provides diploma so students can graduate on time.
Receiving district:				
Enrolls student even if additional immunizations are required (grace period of 30 days). Allows student to remain in kindergarten or first-grade placements even if entry-age requirements differ between states.	Honors sending school placement if equivalent program. May evaluate student to ensure proper placement. Allows student to attend classes in district if classes are not equivalent at receiving school. Honors existing IEP, section 504 plan (Rehabilitation Act of 1973) and the Americans with Disabilities Act (ADA, 1990) accommodations and/or modifications (Schuchs-Gopaul, n.d.). Assesses whether courses can be waived if equivalent ones completed.	Allows for excused absences to visit with parent/legal guardian during deployment cycle. Schools have flexibility in approving absences during testing or for those with excessive absences.	Allows attendance in home school during deployment even if the caregiver does not live in attendance area (caregiver provides transportation). Accepts caregiver power of attorney. Facilitates extracurricular activities even if deadlines for tryouts missed—doesn't ensure place.	May waive course requirements for graduation if similar courses already completed. Needs to show reasonable justification for denying a waiver for prior course completion. Exit exams, achievement tests, and other graduation requirements may be accepted from sending state. If district cannot make reasonable accommodations for required courses and exit exams, must work with sending school for students to obtain a diploma from sending school (and graduate on time).

Note. This table summarizes the major provisions of the legislation. Consult the respective language adopted in each state due to some variability in language and interpretation. Adapted from Fenning et al. (2013).

The following section provides two case examples of how the Compact could be put into practice to assist military youth as they transition from one school district and state to another.

Case Examples Illustrating the Application of the Military Interstate Children's Compact

The James Family

The members of the James family includes Kathryn (mother), Isaiah (father), Seth (son, age 17), and Kevin and Trina (fraternal twins, age 12). Kathryn remains on active duty in the Army, and Isaiah retired from the army about 6 months ago to spend more time supporting the family with frequent military transitions. Kathryn is a surgeon, and Isaiah is a surgical nurse. He moonlights as a nurse and is on call at area hospitals. Kathryn has been deployed twice as a surgeon, while Isaiah experienced one deployment as a surgical nurse during his previous military service.

The family has moved five times because of military service, with Seth experiencing four moves and the twins experiencing three moves during their lifetimes. These moves have resulted in four school changes for Seth and three school changes for the twins. Seth is currently in his last semester of his senior year at Willow Grove High School, and the twins are in seventh grade at Morrison Junior High, both in Huntsville, Alabama. The local public school district supports military youth. Trina has an IEP for a learning disability in the area of reading and receives push-in support for 200 minutes per week. The family currently lives in military housing.

Kathryn has just received notice that she will be deployed to a military hospital in Afghanistan in approximately 2 months. The deployment is estimated to last for approximately 18 months, and will occur in a newly assigned military installation. As part of the anticipated deployment, Kathryn has received orders that she will be reassigned to the new military installation near Seattle, Washington. Therefore, she and the family will move once again next month. It is currently March, and the move to Washington will occur right after spring break. Seth has been busy with college applications, waiting for acceptance letters, and with meeting the graduation requirements for his high school in Alabama. Pine Grove Middle School (for Kevin and Trina) and Pleasant Mountain High School (for Seth) will be the receiving schools. Given this case scenario, here are some ways in which the Compact can be applied to assist this fictional family with the transition from Huntsville, Alabama, to Seattle, Washington.

1. For Seth, since he is in his last semester of high school and close to graduation, the sending and receiving schools can collaborate to facilitate acceptance of graduation requirements and exit exams. The sending school can begin this process by providing the family with Seth's unofficial transcripts, followed by submission of the formal transcripts within 10 days. A review of Seth's unofficial transcript received by Pleasant Mountain High

School revealed that Seth had met essentially the same graduation course requirements in Alabama as are required in Washington, with some flexibility in application, based on a review of each state's graduation requirements (Alabama High School Graduation Requirements, 2018; State of Washington, Office of Superintendent of Public Instruction, n.d.). For example, a career preparedness course can substitute for an occupational education course (Alabama High School Graduation Requirements; State of Washington, Office of Superintendent of Public Instruction, 2015). In addition, although Seth has not taken the high school exit exam required by the state of Washington, substitute tests are permitted, including results of the SAT and ACT, as described in the State of Washington, Office of Superintendent of Public Instruction graduation alternatives document (State of Washington, Office of Superintendent of Public Instruction, 2015). The receiving school district, in this case Pleasant Mountain High School, should be in a position to confer a high school diploma to Seth with minor adjustments and the transfer of credits he earned in Alabama. If the receiving school cannot make these adjustments, the sending and receiving schools would need to collaborate, in the spirit of the Compact, by making a plan for the sending school to provide Seth with a diploma so that he can graduate on time.

2. For Kevin and Trina, once the receiving school obtains the twins' unofficial transcripts from Morrison Junior High School, the process of course placement and any instructional supports needed can begin. For Trina, who has an IEP for a learning disability, the receiving school can honor her existing IEP, so that she continues to receive uninterrupted services. The receiving school, Pine Grove Middle School, can conduct evaluations and assessments to ensure that both students are having their educational needs met.

3. The family will be moving with Kathryn to the Seattle area prior to her deployment. The receiving schools have flexibility in approving absences, so that the children can visit with their mother prior to and during the deployment cycle.

This case example illustrates how the Compact can be used to facilitate school transitions when a family moves for military service. The grade requirements, transition needs, and learning issues for each student vary, but the provisions of the Compact allow flexibility in application based on the particular situation and needs of the family. The second fictional case example also illustrates how the Compact assists military families with school transitions.

The Lyons Family

The Lyons family comprises Dana (mother), Elizabeth (daughter, age 5), and Lorraine (Dana's mother), who is very involved with Elizabeth's care and often stays with Dana and Elizabeth for extended periods of time. Elizabeth's dad left the family when she was a young infant, and there is little to no contact with him. Dana is a member of the Army Reserves and works as a social worker at a community agency in upstate New York. Dana has been deployed once for 9 months to Iraq when Elizabeth was 2 years old. Elizabeth lived with Lorraine during the deployment. Dana, Lorrraine, Elizabeth, and the rest of their extended family, including Dana's two sisters, aunt, uncle, and cousins have always been close. Lorraine received a power of attorney to serve as a caregiver for Elizabeth when Dana is not readily available to make decisions for Elizabeth, including educational ones, particularly during deployment. Dana has just received orders that she will need to go for training for approximately 3 months in Delaware with a new reserve unit and might be deployed as a mental health professional after the training, but the deployment decision has not yet been made. The training will begin right after the Christmas and New Year's holidays.

Meanwhile Elizabeth began kindergarten this academic year, turning 5 on September 30. In New York, decisions about school entry are made through the Local Education Association (LEA; Education Commission of the States, 2014). However, in Delaware, the kindergarten entrance age is 5 before August 31 (Education Commission of the States, 2014). The current plan is for Elizabeth to move with her mom to Delaware during the training period and for Lorraine to stay near them in a small apartment, while Elizabeth and Dana live in military-assigned temporary housing, and for Elizabeth to enroll in a local school district that serves families in military-connected housing. Then, if Dana is deployed, Lorraine will care for Elizabeth in Delaware while she attends the receiving school. In this case scenario, the following provisions of the Compact can be of critical assistance for the following issues:

1. The receiving school can allow Elizabeth to stay in kindergarten since she began kindergarten in New York, even though the state of Delaware has an earlier entrance requirement.
2. The receiving school can honor the power of attorney that Lorraine has as a caregiver. The power of attorney will be particularly useful if Dana is deployed and Lorraine assumes the role of sole caregiver.
3. The receiving school can be flexible in approving excused absences during the time leading up to a deployment, if it occurs, and throughout the deployment cycle.

CONCLUSION

This chapter reviewed major federal legislation and guidelines that apply to the educational needs of military families and their children. The chapter does not provide a detailed analysis of the relevant statutes, but outlines the rights that military families have with respect to education, the available resources for their children, and the ways in which school-based mental health professionals can work with them to ensure that the laws that apply to military families are carried out. Having knowledge about the resources available to military families to support their educational, mental health, and behavioral and social–emotional needs stemming from these legislative efforts is important for military families and the school-based professionals who work with them. These resources and the ways to access them are featured in Appendix 7.1.

APPENDIX 7.1. Information on Accessing Special Education and Legal Resources Described in This Chapter

Resource	Short description	Accessible link
Wright and Wright's Wrightslaw	Detailed, comprehensive, factual, and up-to-date information about special education law and educational law	www.wrightslaw.com
Federal Special Education Regulations (DoD, 2015, as cited in Wright & Wright, 2015)	The DoD (2015). *Provision of early intervention and special education services to eligible DoD dependents; final rule.* (published in the Federal Register)	The Wright and Wright's web site links the DoD (2015) federal guidelines on its web site, here: www.wrightslaw.com/info/dodi.regs.2015.pdf
EFMP description with a link to the Exceptional Family Member Program (EFMP) Downloadable Quick Reference Guide	Extensive, detailed information about the military's EFMP. On the Military One Source website	www.militaryonesource.mil/family-and-relationships/special-needs?content_id=282359
The Exceptional Advocate	An electronic newsletter published several times a year with content specific to military families with special-needs members. It provides updated information for families about the EFMP.	www.militaryonesource.mil/the-exceptional-advocate-enewsletter-archives
Military Interstate Children's Compact Commission (Council of State Governments, 2013)	An interactive map that includes the Compact language adopted by each state	https://mic3.net/interactive-map

CHAPTER 8

Conclusions and Future Directions

This concluding chapter briefly draws upon and summarizes the main points from each of the prior chapters to highlight some key recommendations for current and future school psychology practice.

In Chapter 1, a strengths-based and resiliency approach in working with military youth is described (Astor et al., 2011; Park, 2011). MTSS are recommended as the service delivery model through which a strengths-based approach can be used with military youth (Brown-Chidsey & Bickford, 2016). MTSS are rooted in public health models, which have long been advocated as the service delivery models of choice for and with military youth (Gilreath et al., 2014). The chapter highlights the roles and functions that school psychologists can have in delivering an MTSS model to military youth. A case study application of a strengths-based resiliency approach is also presented. Based on the discussion in the chapter and on the case study, the following key recommendations are offered.

- In order to adapt a strengths-based MTSS model that is effective with military youth, MTSS need to be robust and work for all students in a school population, beginning with Tier 1 supports that include, by definition, military youth. School psychologists, who have extensive training in data-based decision making, can take the lead in supporting MTSS efforts, beginning with the Tier 1 level and using data that are disaggregated by family military status.

- School psychologists can lead efforts in selecting, implementing, and evaluating Tier 2 and/or Tier 3 supports with military youth and families. The interventions and supports for behavioral, mental health, social, and academic needs could be selected on the basis of how best to assist the particular military youth and families one is working with.

- MTSS supports and interventions that can adapted for military youth are ample, yet more work is needed. School psychologists can help to advance our understanding of the practical implementation of MTSS with military youth, particularly by looking at universal (Tier 1) data disaggregated for this group. Specific to military families, Cozza et al. (2014) stress the need for developmental research with military-connected children. Since school psychologists work in the school environments in which military students of all ages are found, they are well positioned to build upon and evaluate models of resiliency that incorporate systems and developmental timing of military-related family experiences (Masten, 2013b) and the MTSS already being implemented in the field. They are also uniquely qualified to lead by virtue of their training and skills acquired in data-based decision making (NASP, 2020). Consider this short fictional snapshot as an illustration of these points.

Ms. Leahy is a school psychologist who works in two schools, one elementary and the other a middle school, located in Rapid City, South Dakota. Her school district is the catchment area for an Air Force base that has a large military presence in the community. The military is a large employer in the region. For the purposes of this example, let's say that roughly 30% of the students in her elementary school and 20% of students in the middle school are connected with the military. Her school district is implementing MTSS for academics at the elementary school. The elementary and middle schools have positive behaviorial interventions and support (PBIS) systems in place at the universal level. Ms. Leahy serves on both the universal academic MTSS team and leads the universal PBIS team at her elementary school. She reviews disaggregated behavioral and academic data for the military students, so she can collaborate with her colleagues to make decisions about how well the MTSS and the behavioral systems are working for all students, including those connected with the military. The universal academic and behavioral data are shared with all parents at conference time to keep families informed, and Ms. Leahy is available to talk with parents, including providing supports for military families who may need help understanding the data as they make educational decisions for their children when preparing to relocate. She also works with her colleagues to develop a welcoming program for military youth transitioning to her district and evaluates the program using existing data, student interviews, and phone calls with family members.

Chapter 2 provides an overview of the various school settings in which military children are educated and examines the cultural contexts of each one. As detailed in the chapter, although the vast majority of school-age children connected with the military attend Civilian schools (School Superintendents Association, 2019), they are educated in a variety of school settings, including DoD and non-DoD schools, each of which has a potential impact on them and their families. Based on the chapter content, consider the following key takeaways and applications.

- School psychologists should educate themselves about the range of school settings in which military-connected children are educated. Such knowledge is essential in order for them to help military youth transition as part of military moves, which may involve navigating from Civilian to DoD installations in domestic as well as international settings. An understanding of such contexts is needed for school psychologists to be knowledgeable enough to support military youth and their families as they make decisions about which schools may be the best choice or about what other options are available to them.

- School psychologists also need to learn more about the different schools that military youth attend to effectively consult with other school professionals. This consultation can take a variety of forms, ranging from psychoeducation delivered in workshops to engaging in school-based consultation with individual students who are leaving one school and transferring into another one.

- Moreover, school psychologists can contribute to the research base by building upon an understanding of how military students fare academically, socially, and in terms of wellness and mental health in varied school environments (e.g., DoD, non-DoD). Arguably, there are more systematic academic outcome data about military youth in DoD settings compared with Civilian ones (Towhey, 2018). School psychologists who work in Civilian schools are well qualified to add to the knowledge base of military youth performance in Civilian schools, and how we can do a better job of supporting them.

Chapter 3 focuses more intensely on how MTSS (Brown-Chidsey & Andren, 2013; McIntosh & Goodman, 2016) can be adapted with military youth along a continuum of supports. Many school psychologists have an identified role in MTSS problem-solving efforts within their schools, and ensuring that military youth are included is a natural evolution. MTSS teams can specifically focus on the systematic review of screening and progress monitoring data disaggregated for military students, whether the data pertain to behavioral, social–emotional, and/or academic issues. The following key takeaways from the chapter are offered as part of this important MTSS role.

- School psychologists who are knowledgeable about military culture and take a strengths-based approach in working with military families are critical to MTSS teams. They can help teams use disaggregated military data across all tiers in a way that is effective, supportive, and not deficit based. They can recommend evidence-supported approaches that have potential benefits for military students. Further, they have a powerful voice in ensuring that data are collected and used effectively to make decisions about continuing, modifying, or eliminating interventions that are not effective or no longer needed.

- By focusing their school-, district-, and state-level efforts on meaningfully using accountability findings disaggregated for military students now mandated under the ESSA (2015), school psychologists can be pivotal in improving MTSS and providing more efficient and inclusive supports for military students, using already mandated data that states now require school districts to collect under the ESSA. Given the new military-identifier requirement under the ESSA (Kowalski, 2015), school psychologists have an excellent opportunity to use these data to track the performance of military youth in Civilian settings and the educational outcomes they achieve. School psychologists can also determine what additional data are needed and should be incorporated into universal screening and/or interventions that are delivered across tiers of support.

Consider another fictional example of one way that school psychologists can use their data-based decision-making skills in supporting military students in a Civilian school.

Mr. Romans works as a school psychologist in a high school just outside of Des Moines, Iowa, that serves military families stationed at a local army base. The base provides training to army military personnel and the National Guard. Mr. Romans leads the school's MTSS team and serves on a districtwide team with a job of coordinating ESSA data collection and other accountability measures across the district. He capitalizes on the opportunity to look at universal/schoolwide data (e.g., ESSA statewide testing and other district benchmark data, such as the percentage of students taking AP courses, AP exam scores, and the credits accrued) disaggregated by family military status to evaluate the performance of military students. Based on these data, he and his team make recommendations for how tiered supports can be delivered to all students, including military youth, at either at the universal, secondary, and/or tertiary level.

Chapter 4 provides a developmental perspective on how schools can promote the healthy social development of youth who are connected with the military across elementary, middle, and high school environments. School psychologists can substantially contribute to this work by applying social developmental theory (e.g., Bowlby, 1969; Erikson, 1999) to better understand how military youth meet social developmental milestones (Cozza et al., 2014). Using social developmental theory as a framework for how military youth navigate social expectations as part of their overall development contributes to the field through a strengths-based rather than a pathologized approach toward military youth (Cozza et al., 2014). Consider the following take-home points tied to the content of the chapter.

- School psychologists are well placed to focus their efforts on how to support the social development of military-connected students using already established social supports that exist along an MTSS continuum (Brown-Chidsey & Andren, 2013) and to consider what additional supports, if any, they need when transitioning to a new school setting as part of a military move.
- School psychologists, using their solid understanding of child development and the social development milestones that are navigated over time, can provide informed psychoeducation and consultation with teachers, administrators, parents, and caregivers. Knowing the social supports and opportunities, such as camp experiences, that military youth can participate in with peers who have similar experiences (such as those provided in Table 4.2) is important information to have on hand, share with others, and update on a regular basis.

- School psychologists can also advocate for elevating military youth and families through assemblies that honor their service. They can encourage military youth to take a leadership role in sharing their unique experiences and honor them in the social context of the school and district.

In Chapter 5, the resiliency model advocated throughout the book (Astor et al., 2013; Park, 2011) is viewed as a helpful framework with which to conceptualize the mental health and wellness of military families. Using a resiliency rather than a deficit lens avoids "pathologizing" military youth, who have enormous strengths, yet may need the right mental health supports at the proper time. It is incumbent upon school psychologists and other mental health professionals to offer such supports while navigating the realities of military students' lives, such as frequent transitions and deployments. In this context, consider the following key recommendations that are aligned with Chapter 5.

- Military youth should naturally and by definition be provided with universal Tier 1 schoolwide supports that foster a welcoming school climate and community (Gilreath et al., 2014; National School Climate Center, 2015). Military youth may need special attention in order to access such supports, given that they may miss these opportunities because of frequent transitions. School psychologists can ensure that military students are identified and acknowledged as universal systems of support are developed with them in mind and ensure that social connections, a positive school climate, and a sense of belonging, are prioritized.

- School psychologists need to learn about and help their colleagues better understand the deployment cycle (Chandra et al., 2011), which may understandably be a particularly stressful time for military families. It is important that whatever supports may be needed are facilitated and that military youth not be pathologized during a time of deployment or at any time.

- Consistent with the content of Chapter 5 and throughout the book, providing mental health and wellness supports could include a school psychologist leading an MTSS team that conducts social–emotional screening of students schoolwide, analyzing data for all students and for specific subgroups, including military youth (Albers & Kettler, 2014). The MTSS team can make decisions about how best to provide resources and supports along a continuum.

- School psychologists can support military youth and families during the most tragic of times, such as the serious injury or death of a service member. With training and expertise in trauma-focused supports (Cohen et al., 2014) and grief (Kaplow et al., 2013), they can deliver direct services and/or coordinate them with community-based and/or military supports.

Consider the following fictional snapshot of how a school psychologist working at the high school level could embed social-emotional and trauma-informed MTSS supports with military students through systemic social-emotional screening and tiered supports.

Mr. Jones is a school psychologist who works at a large suburban high school outside of Chicago, Illinois. The school district serves families who are part of a naval base that provides training for those in the National Guard and also families who are stationed at the base for longer periods of time (typically about 1 to 2 years). The school and larger district have a PBIS system that has taken more time to implement at the high school level, but there has been some progress in developing behavioral expectations. The school is also starting to conduct social–emotional screening, incorporating some items on indicators of trauma, and are piloting the screening this year. Mr. Jones is in charge of the social–emotional screening effort and working with a team that is reviewing the social–emotional and behavioral supports that are available. This will be an ongoing multiyear process that will need to be revisited. He will be working with his team to disaggregate the social–emotional screening data by military status when the information is collected in September and to lead subsequent more in-depth safety assessments and interviews. Mr. Jones is working with his team to ensure that behavioral expectations are taught and the PBIS system is reviewed with military students when they transition to the school. He is also setting up a buddy system for military youth that transition in, and facilitates a group for military youth focused on socialization, transition, and adjustment to the school. In collaboration with community-service providers and a health clinic, he facilitates the ADAPT (Gewirtz, 2013) program for families with a service member who will deploy, is deployed, or is back from a deployment. He uses the data collected on trauma and other indicators to offer trauma-focused CBT with military youth in the school either directly or by referrals to trusted community service providers with the consent and agreement of the family members. He is also on the wraparound planning team, which includes several military families.

As noted in Chapter 6, children in military families experience an average of nine school transitions (Sanchez, 2012, as cited in Fenning et al., 2013). Here again, school psychologists are best prepared to assist with transitions and to foster the academic success of military youth. Here are some key takeaways for how academic transitions could be supported.

• School psychologists should take the time to educate themselves about what is involved when a military family's living situation changes—essentially by being humble and open to hearing from the families what their needs are so that their transition is a smooth one. School psychologists can then provide professional development and in-service training with fellow educators and families both connected with and not connected with the military, who can serve as allies. Simply having basic information about the many websites and resources available from organizations committed to supporting military families given in Chapter 6 (Table 6.1) is a starting point.

• School psychologists also work with military students who have special education needs or disabilities as members of IEP teams, and can be particularly helpful in supporting those who have diverse learning needs that make transitions and orientations to a new routine potentially challenging. For example, by paying particular attention to any changing needs of military youth, school psychologists can advocate for a modification to MTSS, the IEP, or the behavior intervention plan.

- School psychologists are in an excellent position to advance research into best practices that support military youth in their academic transitions. One gap in the military-student transition literature is a solid understanding about how the developmental age of military youth influences the transition (Cozza et al., 2014). Further research is needed about what role the demographics (e.g., percentage of military student population) of the sending and receiving schools play in the academic transition of military youth.

Consider the following fictional snapshot application of the topic discussed in Chapter 6:

> Ms. Bryant is a school psychologist who works in the Fort Sam Houston Independent School District, a public school district specifically for military youth in Texas. The school district serves military families in the very large Fort Sam Houston and Camp Bullis army bases. Fort Sam Houston is one of the largest military medical training installations in the country. The school district is located on a military base. Ms. Bryant is one of four psychologists who serves two elementary schools, one of which has an early childhood program. She also organizes Child Find in the district, including early childhood screenings. Ms. Bryant, along with a social worker at the school, Mr. Sims, are the points of contact for military families in the district. With the knowledge that many military families will transition into school districts that do not have a high percentage of military families, Ms. Bryant and Mr. Sims work closely with military families in identifying EFMP support staff (when necessary for students with disabilities) and the school liaison office in the receiving district. The transition of all students is carefully thought through, particularly for students with disabilities like autism, which require special attention to ensure they go smoothly. Together they prepare for a "warm handoff" by reaching out to others who can help military families in the receiving district. Because they are well versed in the Compact, they also provide consultation and psychoeducation about it with military families and the receiving staff in new locations that might not be as familiar with it. Ms. Bryant pays particular attention to military youth in early childhood settings and strives to avoid any disruption in services, to the degree possible, when military families relocate.

Chapter 7 highlights the relevant legislation that applies to school-age military youth, primarily the new mandates in the ESSA (2015) that now require each state to collect accountability assessment data disaggregated for military students. These reporting and analysis requirements could have enormous potential for our field to better understand the academic lives of military youth and how to better support them. School psychologists, as the data-based experts, can take a leadership role in using these data not just for a reporting function, but as a way to improve upon interventions and practices for and with military youth.

Arguably, the Compact (Military Interstate Children's Compact Commission, 2015) can significantly help military youth whose families frequently move across districts, state lines, and into international settings (Sanchez, 2012, as cited in Fenning et al., 2013). Table 7.1 provides an overview of the major tenets of the Compact and the responsibilities of the sending and receiving districts in complying with it. We offer some key future directions from the chapter.

To date, there is significant variability in how these data are captured in state education agency data systems (Mesecar & Soifer, 2018). School psychologists can be integral in advocating for efficient data collection systems at the state, district, and school level to meaningfully inform practices and interventions with military youth. They can weigh in at the state and school-system level to advocate for the best data collection systems and provide models and examples from the field as to how these data can be used to improve service delivery with military youth.

It is imperative that school psychologists have a thorough knowledge of the Compact and share it with fellow educators, military families, students, and the broader community beyond the schools. They can provide technical assistance to their colleagues by sharing their experiences with using the Compact as an advocacy tool, and can collaborate with others to apply it in practice, documenting positive outcomes and challenges. The on-the-ground experiences of school psychologists, educators, and military families are needed to inform policy at the local, state, national, and international level.

Related to this point, school psychologists can engage in research that centers on evaluating the degree to which the Compact addresses the challenges and nuances of family moves and transitions. This research can be done through a variety of research methodologies, such as quantitative (e.g., surveys, evaluation of academic performance and indicators) and qualitative (e.g., interviews with families and students) methodologies and through case study examples that school psychologists have access to in their practice.

Future directions in the field could be initially focused on developing case examples. Then more rigorous evaluations of the implementation of the Compact could be conducted as it becomes more established in state education agency regulations. ESSA military-identifier outcome data and other accountability measures could be analyzed across time, as well as formative assessment tools that are collected at the school and/or district level as part of MTSS implementation (e.g., CBM outcomes or measures of academic progress testing).

OVERALL SUMMARY AND CONCLUDING COMMENTS

As stated throughout the book, military youth and their families bring enormous strengths and resiliency to any setting they are in, including schools (Park, 2011). The primary focus of this book was to draw out these strengths and to provide information and resources to support military youth and their families in the academic, mental health, and social arenas. It was also written to provide information about best practices during key and potentially trying times in the lives of military families, such as during military moves, in deployment situations, and in situations of severe injury or death. By virtue of their unique position as highly trained school-based mental health professionals (NASP, 2015) who work in the

Civilian public schools, DoD-operated schools, and international institutions that educate military students, school psychologists can be outstanding advocates for military students.

Along with other school-based mental health professionals, such as counselors and school social workers, school psychologists can partner with educators, school administrators, and the larger community in honoring the service of military families. We all owe a debt of gratitude for this service, and I hope the content of this book provides relevant information and resources to support school psychologists and other school personnel in their work with military families. We owe it as a nation to make the school experience the best it can possibly be for military youth and their families as one small token of appreciation for their service to the country and the world.

References

Adelman, H. S. (1996). Restructuring education support services and integrating community resources: Beyond the full service school model. *School Psychology Review, 25*(4), 431–445.

Adelman, H. S., & Taylor, T. (2012). Mental health in schools: Moving in new directions. *Contemporary School Psychology, 16*, 9–18.

Alabama State Department of Education. (2018). *Alabama high school graduation requirements.* Alabama Administrative Code 290-3-1-02(8) and (8)(a). Montgomery, AL: Author. Retrieved from *www.alsde.edu/sec/sct/Graduation%20Information/AHSG%20Requirements%20May%202018.pdf.*

Albers, C. A., & Kettler, R. J. (2014). Best practices in universal screening. In P. L. Harrison & A. Thomas (Eds.), *Best practices in school psychology* (pp. 121–132). Bethesda, MD: National Association of School Psychologists.

Algozzine, B., Wang, C., & Violette, A. S. (2011). Reexamining the relationship between academic achievement and social behavior. *Journal of Positive Behavior Interventions, 13*, 3–16.

Allen, K. (2011). Cognitive-behavioral therapy in the school setting: Expanding the school psychologist's toolkit. *Psychology in the Schools, 48*(3), 215–222.

American Association of School Administrators. (2009a, November 16). How schools can support the military child [Video file]. Retrieved from *www.youtube.com/watch?v=Dyua5DlQNn4*

American Association of School Administrators. (2009b). *AASA Toolkit: Supporting the military child: Guidance for school leaders on meeting the unique educational needs of children whose parents are deployed or in transition.* Arlington, VA: Author. Retrieved from *www.aasa.org/uploadedFiles/Resources/Toolkits/Other_Toolkits/AASA_Supporting_the_Military_Child_Toolkit/MilitaryChildToolkitComplete.pdf.*

American Psychological Association Division 19. (2016). The Society for Military Psychology. Retrieved from *www.apadivisions.org/division-19.*

Americans with Disabilities Act of 1990, Public Law 101-336, §2, 104 Stat. 328 (1991).

Arnold, P., Garner, J., Neale-McFall, C., & Nunnery, J. (2011). *Needs of military-connected school divisions in southeastern Virginia.* Norfolk, VA: Center for Educational Partnerships at Old Dominion University.

Aronson, K. R., Caldwell, L. L., Perkins, D. F., & Pasch, K. W. (2011). Assisting children and families with military-related disruptions: The United States Marine Corps School Liaison Program. *Psychology in the Schools, 48*(10), 998–1015.

Astor, R. A. (2011). The need to support students from military families. *Education Week, 30*(33), 27, 32. Retrieved from *www.edweek.org/ew/articles/2011/06/08/33astor_ep.h30.html*.

Astor, R., De Pedro, K., Gilreath, T., Esqueda, M., & Benbenishty, R. (2013). The promotional role of school and community contexts for military students. *Clinical Child and Family Psychology Review, 16*(3), 233–244.

Astor, R. A., Jacobson, L., Benbenishty, R., Pineda, D., & Atuel, H. (2012a). *The teacher's guide for supporting students from military families.* New York: Teachers College Press.

Astor, R. A., Jacobson, L., Benbenishty, R., Pineda, D., & Atuel, H. (2012b). *The school administrator's guide for supporting students from military families.* New York: Teachers College Press.

Astor, R. A., Jacobson, L., Benbenishty, R., Pineda, D., & Atuel, H. (2012c). *The pupil personnel guide for supporting students from military families.* New York: Teachers College Press.

Astor, R. A., Jacobson, L., Benbenishty, R., Pineda, D., & Atuel, H. (2012d). *The military family's parent guide for supporting your child in school.* New York: Teachers College Press.

Austin, G., Bates, S., & Duerr, M. (2013a). *Guidebook for the California Healthy Kids Survey: Part I. Administration.* San Francisco: West Ed.

Austin, G., Bates, S., & Duerr, M. (2013b). *Guidebook to the California Healthy Kids Survey: Part II. Survey content.* San Francisco: WestEd. Retrieved from *https://chks.wested.org/resources/chks_guidebook_2_coremodules.pdf*.

Baker-Smith, K., & Moore, K. A. (2001). Early onset of social anxiety: Impact on Erikson's stages of psychosocial development. In K. A. Moore (Ed.), *Relationships: Their impact on social and mental well-being* (pp. 19–23). Melbourne: Australian Psychological Society.

Bal, A., King Thorius, K., & Kozleski, E. (2012). *Culturally responsive positive behavioral support matters.* Tempe, AZ: Equity Alliance at Arizona State University. Retrieved from *www.equityallianceatasu.org/sites/defautfilesCRPBIS_Matters.pdf*.

Barker, L. H., & Berry, K. D. (2009). Developmental issues impacting military families with young children during single and multiple deployments. *Military Medicine, 174*(10), 1033–1040.

Batsche, G. (2007). *Problem solving and response to intervention: Focusing on improved academic achievement for all students.* Ft. Lauderdale: Florida Association of School Nurses.

Bohanon, H., Fenning, P., Carney, K., Minnis, M., Anderson-Harris, S., Moroz, K., et al. (2006). School-wide application of urban high school positive behavior support: A case study. *Journal of Positive Behavior Interventions, 8,* 131–145.

Bowlby, J. (1969). *Attachment and loss: Vol. 1. Attachment.* New York: Basic Books.

Bradshaw, C. P., Sudhinaraset, M., Mmari, D., Blum, R. W. (2010). School transitions among military adolescents: A qualitative study of stress and coping. *School Psychology Review, 39*(1), 84–105.

Brendel, K. E., Maynard, B. R., Albright, D. L., & Bellomo, M. (2014). Effects of school-based interventions with U.S. military-connected children: A systematic review. *Research on Social Work Practice, 24*(6), 649–658.

Bridglall, B. L., & Gordon, E. W. (2003). Raising minority academic achievement: The Department of Defense model. *Pedagogical Inquiry and Praxis, 5.*

Brown, R., Steege, M. W., & Bickford, R. (2014). Responsive assessment and instruction practices. In S. G. Little & A. Akin-Little (Eds.), *Academic assessment and intervention* (pp. 161–178). New York: Routledge.

Brown-Chidsey, R., & Andren, K. J. (Eds.). (2013). *Assessment for intervention: A problem-solving approach* (2nd ed.). New York: Guilford Press.

Brown-Chidsey, R., & Bickford, R. (2016). *Practical handbook of multi-tiered systems of support: Building academic and behavioral success in schools.* New York: Guilford Press.

Bruns, E. J., Walker, J. S., Adams, J., Miles, P., Osher, T. W., Rast, J., et al. (2004). *Ten principles of the wraparound process*. Portland, OR: National Wraparound Initiative, Research and Training Center on Family Support and Children's Mental Health, Portland State University.

Brunwasser, S. M., Gillham, J. E., & Kim, E. S. (2009). A meta-analytic review of the Penn Resiliency Program's effect on depressive symptoms. *Journal of Consulting and Clinical Psychology, 77*(6), 1042–1054.

Buchanan, T. (2014). Operation Purple Camps: Relevant now and then. *Journal of Applied Research on Children: Informing Policy for Children at Risk, 5*(1), Article 25.

Burns, M. K., & Gibbons, K. (2012). *Implementing response-to-intervention in elementary and secondary schools: Procedures to assure scientific-based practice* (2nd ed.). New York: Routledge.

Campbell, C. L., Brown, E. J., & Okwara, L. (2011). Addressing sequelae of trauma and interpersonal violence in military children: A review of the literature and case illustration. *Cognitive and Behavioral Practice, 18*, 131–143.

Caraballo, L., Lozenski, B., Lyiscott, J., & Morrell, E. (2017). YPAR and critical epistemologies: Rethinking education research. *Review of Research in Education, 41*(1), 311–336.

Castillo, J. M., & Batsche, G. M. (2012). Scaling up response to intervention: The influence of policy and research and the role of program evaluation. *NASP Communiqué, 40*(8), 14–16.

Centers for Disease Control and Prevention. (2009). *School connectedness: Strategies for increasing protective factors among youth*. Atlanta: U.S. Department of Health and Human Services.

Chandra, A., Burns, R. M., Tanielian, T., Jaycox, L. H., & Scott, M. M. (2008). *Understanding the impact of deployment on children and families: Findings from a Pilot Study of Operation Purple Camp Participants* (RAND Center for Military Health Policy Research Working Paper No. WR-566). Santa Monica, CA: RAND Corporation.

Chandra, A., Lara-Cinisomo, S., Jaycox, L. H., Tanielian, T., Han, B., Burns, R. M., et al. (2011). *Views from the homefront: The experiences of youth and spouses from military families*. Santa Monica, CA: RAND Corporation.

Chandra, A., & London, A. S. (2013). Unlocking insights about military children and families. *The Future of Children, 23*(2), 187–188.

Clever, M., & Segal, D. R. (2013). The demographics of military children and families. *The Future of Children, 23*(2), 13–39.

Cohen, J. A., & Mannarino, A. P. (2011). Trauma-focused CBT for traumatic grief in military children. *Journal of Contemporary Psychotherapy, 41*, 219–227.

Cohen, J. A., Mannarino, A. P., & Cozza, S. J. (2014). Trauma-focused cognitive behavioral therapy for military families: An implementation manual. Retrieved from *https://tfcbt.org/wp-content/uploads/2018/05/Military-implementation-manual.pdf.*

Cohen, J. A., Mannarino, A. P., & Deblinger, E. (2010). Trauma-focused cognitive behavioral therapy for traumatized children. In J. R. Weisz & A. E. Kazdin (Eds.), *Evidence-based psychotherapies for children and adolescents* (2nd ed., pp. 295–311). New York: Guilford Press.

Cohen, J. A., Mannarino, A. P., & Deblinger, E. (2012). *Trauma-focused CBT for children and adolescents: Treatment applications.* New York: Guilford Press.

Cohen, S., Kamarck, T., & Mermelstein, R. (1983). A global measure of perceived stress. *Journal of Health and Social Behavior, 24,* 385–396.

Collaborative for Academic, Social, and Emotional Learning. (2012). *2013 CASEL guide: Effective social and emotional learning programs—Preschool and elementary school edition.* Chicago: Author.

Collaborative for Academic, Social, and Emotional Learning. (2015). *2015 CASEL guide: Effective social and emotional learning programs—Middle and high school edition.* Chicago: Author.

Council for Exceptional Children. (2015). CEC's summary of selected provisions in Every Student Succeeds Act (ESSA). Retrieved from *www.policyinsider.org/2015/12/want-to-know-more-about-essa.html.*

Council of State Governments. (2008). Interstate compact on educational opportunity for military children: Legislative resource kit. Retrieved from *www.csg.org/knowledgecenter/docs/ncic/RESOURCEKIT-January2008final.pdf.*

Council of State Governments. (2013). Military Interstate Children's Compact Commission (MIC3) FAQ. Retrieved from *http://mic3.net.*

Cox, J., Davies, D. R., Burlingame, G. M., Campbell, J. E., Layne, C. M., & Katzenbach, R. J. (2007). Effectiveness of a trauma/grief-focused group intervention: A qualitative study with war-exposed Bosnian adolescents. *International Journal of Group Psychotherapy, 57,* 319–345.

Cozza, S. J., Lerner, R. M., & Haskins, R. (2014). Military and veteran families and children: Policies and programs for health maintenance and positive development. *Social Policy Report, 28*(3), 1–29.

Crick, N. R., & Bigbee, M. A. (1998). Relational and overt forms of peer victimization: A multi-informant approach. *Journal of Consulting and Clinical Psychology, 66*(2), 337–347.

Cusumano, D. L., Algozzine, K., & Algozzine, B. (2014). Multi-tiered system of supports for effective inclusion in elementary schools. In J. McLesky, N. L. Waldron, F. Spooner, & B. Algozzine (Eds.), *Handbook of effective inclusive schools: Research and practice,* (pp. 183–196). New York: Routledge.

Davis, J. M., & Finke, E. H. (2015). The experience of military families with children with autism spectrum disorders during relocation and separation. *Journal of Autism and Developmental Disorders, 45,* 2019–2034.

Deno, S. L. (1985). Curriculum-based measurement: The emerging alternative. *Exceptional Children, 52*(3), 219–232.

De Pedro, K., Astor, R. A., Benbenishty, R., Estrada, J. N., Smith, G. R., & Esqueda, M. C. (2011). The children of military service members: Challenges, resources, and future educational research. *Review of Educational Research, 81*(4), 566–618.

De Pedro, K., Astor, R. A., Gilreath, T. D., Benbenishty, R., & Esqueda, M. C. (2014). School climate perceptions among students in military connected schools: A comparison of military and non-military students in the same schools. *Military Behavior Health Journal, 2*(1), 3–13.

De Pedro, K. T., Esqueda, M. C., Cederbaum, J. A., & Astor, R. A. (2014). District, school, and community stakeholder perspectives on the experiences of military-connected students. *Teachers College Record, 116,* 1–32.

Dever, B. V., Kamphaus, R. W., Dowdy, E., Raines, T. C., & DiStefano, C. (2013). Surveillance of middle and high school mental health risk by student self-report screener. *Western Journal of Emergency Medicine, 14*(4), 384–390.

Dowdy, E., Doane, K., Eklund, K., & Dever, B. V. (2011). A comparison of teacher nomination and screening to identify behavioral and emotional risk within a sample of underrepresented students. *Journal of Emotional and Behavioral Disorders, 21*(2), 127–137.

Easterbrooks, M. A., Ginsburg, K., & Lerner, R. M. (2013). Resilience among military youth. *The Future of Children, 23*(2), 99–120.

Eccles, J. S. (1999). The development of children ages 6 to 14. *The Future of Children, 9*(2), 30–44.

Education Commission of the States. (2014). *50 state comparison. Kindergarten entrance age.* Denver, CO: Author. Retrieved from *http://ecs.force.com/mbdata/mbquestRT?rep=Kq1402*.

Erikson, E. (1963). *Childhood and society.* New York: Norton.

Esposito-Smythers, C., Wolff, J., Lemmon, K. M., Bodzy, M., Swenson, R. R., & Spirito, A. (2011). Military youth and deployment cycle: Emotional health consequences and recommendations for intervention. *Journal of Family Psychology, 25*(4), 497–507.

Esqueda, M. C., Astor, R. A., & De Pedro, K. T. (2012). A call to duty: Educational policy and school reform addressing the needs of children from military families. *Educational Researcher, 41*(2), 65–70.

Every Student Succeeds Act of 2015, Public Law 114-95 § 114 Stat. 1177 (2015–2016).

Fenning, P., Harris, A., & Viellieu, L. (2013). Supporting the school success of children from military families: The role of school psychologists, *The School Psychologist, 67*(3), 16–24.

Flake, E. M., Davis, B. E., Johnson, P. L., & Middleton, L. (2009). The psychosocial effects of deployment on military children. *Journal of Developmental and Behavioral Pediatrics, 30*(4), 271–278.

Friedberg, R. D., & Brelsford, G. M. (2011). Using cognitive behavioral therapy to help children cope with parental military deployments. *Journal of Contemporary Psychotherapy, 41*, 229–236.

Friedberg, R. D., & McClure, J. M. (2015). *Clinical practice of cognitive therapy with children and adolescents: The nuts and bolts* (2nd ed.). New York: Guilford Press.

Garcia, E., De Pedro, K. T., Astor, R. A. Lester, P., & Benbenishty, R. (2015). FOCUS school-based skill building groups: Training and implementation. *Journal of Social Work Education, 51*(Suppl. 1), 102–116.

Gewirtz, A. (2013). *Evaluation of a web-enhanced parenting program for military families: After Deployment, Adaptive Parenting Tools (ADAPT).* Washington, DC: Friends of NIDA Congressional Briefing.

Gewirtz, A. H., Polusny, M. A., Forgatch, M., DeGarmo, D., & Marquez, B. (2009). *Effectiveness of a web-enhanced parenting program for military families.* Grant No. DA030114 awarded to the University of Minnesota from the National Institutes of Health, National Institute on Drug Abuse.

Gillham, J. E., Hamilton, J., Freres, D. R., Patton, K., & Gallop, R. (2006). Preventing depression among early adolescents in the primary care setting: A randomized controlled study of the Penn Resiliency Program. *Journal of Abnormal Child Psychology, 34*, 203–219.

Gillham, J. E., Reivich, K. J., & Jaycox, L. H. (2008). *The Penn Resiliency Program.* Unpublished manuscript, University of Pennsylvania, Philadelphia, PA.

Gilreath, T. D., Estrada, J. N., Pineda, D., Benbenishty, R., & Astor, R. A. (2014). Development and use of the California Healthy Kids Survey Military Module to support students in military-connected schools. *Children and Schools, 36*(1), 23–29.

Goodman, R. (1997). The Strengths and Difficulties Questionnaire: A research note. *Journal of Child Psychology and Psychiatry, 38*, 581–586.

Hall, L. K. (2008). *Counseling military families: What mental health professionals need to know.* New York: Routledge.

Hall, L. K. (2011). The importance of understanding military culture. *Social Work in Health Care, 50*(1), 4–18.

Hernández Finch, M. E. (2012). Special considerations with response to intervention and instruction for students with diverse backgrounds. *Psychology in the Schools, 49*(3), 285–296.

Hisle-Gorman, E., Harrington, D., Nylund, C. M., Tercyak, K P., Anthony, B. J., & Gorman, G. H. (2015). Impact of parents' wartime military deployment and injury on young children's safety and mental health. *Journal of American Academy of Child and Adolescent Psychiatry, 54*(4), 294–301.

Horner, R. H., Sugai, G., & Anderson, C. M. (2010). Examining the evidence base for school-wide positive behavior support. *Focus on Exceptionality, 42*(8), 1–14.

Horner, R. H., Todd, A. W., Lewis-Palmer-T., Irvin, L. K., Sugai, G., & Boland, J. B. (2004). School-wide Evaluation Tool (SET): A research instrument for assessing school-wide positive behavior supports. *Journal of Positive Behavior Interventions, 6*(1), 3–12.

Huberty, T. J. (2012). *Anxiety and depression in children and adolescents: Assessment, intervention and prevention.* New York: Springer.

Huebner, A. J., Mancini, J. A., Wilcox, R. M., Grass, S. R., & Grass, G. A. (2007). Parental deployment and youth in military families: Exploring uncertainty and ambiguous loss. *Family Relations, 56*, 112–122.

Illinois State Board of Education. (2019a). 5 Essentials Survey. Retrieved from *www.isbe.net/Pages/5Essentials-Survey.aspx*.

Illinois State Board of Education. (2019b). State template for the consolidated state plan under the Every Student Succeeds Act. Retrieved from *www.isbe.net/Documents/ESSA-Amendment1-redline.pdf*.

Illinois State Board of Education. (n.d.). Illinois Learning Standards Social/Emotional Learning. Retrieved from *www.isbe.net/ils/social_emotional/standards.htm*.

Individuals with Disabilities Education Act (IDEA), 20 U.S.C. §1400 (2004).

Interstate Commission on Educational Opportunity for Military Children Rules. (2012). *Military Interstate Children's Compact Commission.* Lexington, KY: Author. Retrieved from *http://mic3.net/pages/resources/documents/MIC3CommissionRules-Final-amendedNov2012_000.pdf*.

Intervention Central. (n.d.). Tier 1/schoolwide screening: Assessing the entire school population for academic risk. Retrieved from *www.interventioncentral.org/response_to_intervention_school_wide_screening*.

Israel, A. C., Roderick, H. A., & Ivanova, M. Y. (2002). A measure of the stability of activity in a family environment. *Journal of Psychopathology and Behavioral Assessment, 24*, 85–95.

Jagger, J. C., & Lederer, S. (2014). Impact of geographic mobility on military children's access to special education services. *Children & Schools, 36*(1), 15–22.

Jellinek, M. S., Murphy, J. M., Robinson, J., Feins, A., Lamb, S., & Fenton, T. (1988). Pediatric Symptom Checklist: Screening school-age children for psychosocial dysfunction. *Journal of Pediatrics, 112*, 201–209.

Jenkins, J., Schulze, M., Marti, A., & Harbaugh, A. G. (2017). Curriculum-based measurement of reading growth: Weekly versus intermittent progress monitoring. *Exceptional Children, 84*(1), 42–54.

Jones, S. M., Barnes, S. P., Bailey, R., & Doolittle, E. J. (2017). Promoting social and emotional competencies in elementary school. *The Future of Children, 27*(1), 49–72.

Jordan, K. F. (2002). Identity formation and the adult third culture kid. In M. G. Ender (Ed.), *Military brats and other global nomads: Growing up in organization families* (pp. 211–228). Westport, CT: Praeger.

Kamphaus, R. W., & Reynolds, C. R. (2007). *BASC-2 Behavior and Emotional Screening System (BASC-2 BESS)*. San Antonio, TX: Pearson.

Kaplow, J. B., Layne, C. M., Saltzman, W. R., Cozza, S. J., & Pynoos, R. S. (2013). Using multidimensional grief theory to explore the effects of deployment reintegration, and death on military youth and families. *Clinical Child Family Psychological Review, 16*, 322–340.

Kilgus, S. P., Chafouleas, S. M., & Riley-Tillman, T. C. (2013). Development and initial validation of the Social and Academic Behavior Risk Screener for elementary grades. *School Psychology Quarterly, 28*, 210–226.

Kim, J., McIntosh, K., & Hoselton, R. (2014). *Do schools with adequate Tier I SWPBIS implementation have stronger implementation at Tiers II and III?* Eugene: OSEP National Technical Assistance Center on Positive Behavioral Interventions and Supports, University of Oregon.

Kitmitto, S., Huberman, M., Blankenship, C., Hannan, S., Norris, D., & Christenson, B. (2011). *Educational options and performance of military connected school districts research study—final report*. San Mateo, CA: American Institutes for Research.

Kovaleski, J. F., & Pederson, J. A. (2014). Best practices in data-analysis teaming. In P. L. Harrison & A. Thomas (Eds.). *Best practices in school psychology* (pp. 99–120). Bethesda, MD: National Association of School Psychologists.

Kowalski, P. (2015). The Every Student Succeeds Act says "YES, Data matters! Retrieved from *http://dataqualitycampaign.org/blog/2015/12/the-every-student-succeeds-act-says-yes-data-matter*.

Kratochwill, T. R., Altschaefl, M. R., & Bice-Urbach, B. (2014). Best practices in school-based problem-solving consultation: Applications in prevention and intervention systems. In P. L. Harrison & A. Thomas (Eds.), *Best practices in school psychology* (pp. 461–482). Bethesda, MD: National Association of School Psychologists.

Kudler, H., & Porter. R. I. (2013). Building communities of care for military children and families. *The Future of Children, 23*(2), 163–181.

Lane, K. L., Oakes, W. P., Carter, E. W., & Messnger, M. (2015). Examining behavioral risk and academic performance for students transitioning from elementary to middle school. *Journal of Positive Behavior Interventions, 17*(1), 39–49.

Lane, K. L., Oakes, W. P., Ennis, R. P., Cox, M. L., Schatschneider, C., & Lambert, W. (2011). Additional evidence for the reliability and validity of the student risk screening scale at the high school level: A replication and extension. *Journal of Emotional and Behavioral Disorders, 21*(2), 97–115.

Layne, C. M., Saltzman, W. R., Kaplow, J. B., & Pynoos, R. S. (2013). *Trauma and grief component therapy for adolescents*. Unpublished treatment manual, University of California, Los Angeles.

Layne, C. M., Saltzman, W. R., Poppleton, L., Burlingame, G. M., Pasalic, A., Durakovic-Belko, E., et al. (2008). Effectiveness of a school-based group psychotherapy program for war-exposed adolescents: A randomized controlled trial. *Journal of the American Academy of Child and Adolescent Psychiatry, 47,* 1048–1062.

Leen-Feldner, E. W., Feldner, M. T., Knapp, A., Bunaciu, L., Blumenthal, H., & Amstadter, A. B. (2013). Offspring psychological and biological correlates of parental posttraumatic stress: Review of the literature and research agenda. *Clinical Psychology Review, 33,* 1106–1133.

Lemmon, K. M., & Chartrand, M. M. (2009). Caring for America's children: Military youth in the time of war. *Pediatrics in Review, 30*(6), e42.

Lerner, R. M., Almerigi, J. B., Theokas, C., & Lerner, J. V. (2005). Positive youth development: A view of the issues. *Journal of Early Adolescence, 25*(1), 10–16.

Lerner, R. M., Zaff, J. F., & Lerner, J. V. (2009). America's military youth: Towards the study of positive development in the face of challenge (Executive summary of a White Paper prepared for the Military Child Education Coalition). Retrieved from *www.militarychild.org/public/upload/images/AMY_ExecSum.pdf.*

Lester, P., Peterson, K., Reeves, J., Knauss, L., Glover, D., Mogil, C., et al. (2010). The Long War and parental combat deployment: Effects on military children and at-home spouses. *Journal of the American Academy of Child and Adolescent Psychiatry, 49*(4), 310–320.

Lester, P., Saltzman, W. R., Woodward, K., Glover, D., Leskin, G. A., Bursch, B., et al. (2012). Evaluation of a family-centered prevention intervention for military children and families facing wartime deployments. *American Journal of Public Health, 102*(Suppl. 1), 548–554.

Lester, P., Stein, J. A., Saltzman, W., Woodward, K., MacDermid, S. W., Milburn, N., et al. (2013). Psychological health of military children: Longitudinal evaluation of a family-centered prevention program to enhance family resilience. *Military Medicine, 178*(8), 838–845.

Lewis, T. J., Barrett, S., Sugai, G., & Horner, R. H. (2010). *Blueprint for schoolwide positive behavior support training and professional development.* Eugene, OR: National Technical Assistance Center Positive Behavior Interventions and Support. Retrieved from *www.pbis.org/common/cms/files/pbisresources/PBIS_PD_Blueprint_v3.pdf.*

Lucier-Greer, M., Arnold, A. L., Grimsley, R. N., Ford, J. L., Bryant, C., & Mancini, J. A. (2016). Parental military service and adolescent well-being: Mental health, social connections and coping among youth in the USA. *Child and Family Social Work, 21*(4), 421–432.

Lucier-Greer, M., Arnold, A. L., Mancini, J. A., Ford, J. L., & Bryant, C. M. (2015). Influences of cumulative risk and protective factors on the adjustment of adolescents in military families. *Family Relations, 64,* 363–377.

Malecki, C. K., Demaray, M. K., & Elliott, S. N. (2000). *The Child and Adolescent Social Support Scale.* Dekalb: Northern Illinois University.

Mansfield, A. J., Kaufman, J. S., Marshall, S. W., Gaynes, B. N., Morrissey, J. P., & Engel, C. C. (2010). Deployment and the use of mental health services among U.S. Army wives. *New England Journal of Medicine, 362,* 101–109.

Marchant, K. H., & Medway, F. J. (1987). Adjustment and achievement associated with mobility in military families. *Psychology in the Schools, 24*(3), 289–294.

Masten, A. S. (2001). Ordinary magic: Resilience processes in development. *American Psychologist, 56*(3), 227–238.

Masten, A. S. (2013a). Afterward: What we can learn from military children and families. *The Future of Children, 23*(2), 199–212.

Masten, A. (2013b). Competence, risk and resilience in military families: A conceptual commentary. *Clinical Child and Family Psychological Review, 16,* 278–281.

McIntosh, K., Flannery, K. B., Sugai, G., Braun, D., & Cochrane, K. (2008). Relationships between academics and problem behavior in the transition from middle school to high school. *Journal of Positive Behavior Interventions, 10*, 243–255.

McIntosh, K., & Goodman, S. (2016). *Integrated multi-tiered systems of support: Blending RTI and PBIS:* New York: Guilford Press.

Medical University of South Carolina. (2017). TF-CBT web 2.0. Retrieved from *https://tfcbt2.musc.edu/en*.

Mesecar, D., & Soifer, D. (2018). *Getting school districts ready for the military student identifier.* Alexandria, VA: Lexington Institute. Retrieved from *https://forstudentsuccess.org/wp-content/uploads/2018/09/MSI-Lex-Report_final.pdf*.

Milburn, N. G., & Lightfoot, M. (2013). Adolescents in wartime U.S. military families: A developmental perspective on challenges and resources. *Clinical Child Family Psychology Review, 16*(3), 266–277.

Military Benefits. (2019). Month of the military child 2019. Retrieved from *https://militarybenefits.info/month-of-the-military-child*.

Military Child Education Coalition. (2012). *Education of the military child in the 21st century: Current dimensions of educational experiences for army children.* Harker Heights, TX: Author.

Military Child Education Coalition. (2015). Retrieved from *www.militarychild.org*.

Military Child Education Coalition. (2019a). Students. Retrieved from *www.militarychild.org/audience/students*.

Military Child Education Coalition. (2019b). Professionals. Retrieved from *www.militarychild.org/audience/professionals*.

Military Child Education Coalition. (2019c). Virtual learning opportunities. Retrieved from *www.militarychild.org/programs/virtual-learning-opportunities*.

Military Child Education Coalition. (n.d). Student identifier. Retrieved from *www.militarychild.org/student-identifier*.

Military Child Education Coalition/Columbia University Center for Public Research and Leadership. (2017). *The challenges of supporting highly mobile, military-connected children in school transitions.* Harker Heights TX: Author. Retrieved from *www.militarychild.org/upload/files/resources/Military_Student_Transitions_Study_2017.pdf*.

Military.com. (2019). DoD Education Activity Schools. Retrieved from *www.military.com/spouse/military-life/military-resources/dod-education-activity-schools.html*.

Military Interstate Children's Compact Commission. (2014). *Guide for parents, school officials and public administrators.* Lexington, KY: Author.

Military Interstate Children's Compact Commission. (2015). MIC3 news, views, and transitions. *Newsletter for the Interstate Commission on Educational Opportunity for Military Children.* Retrieved from *www.mic3.net/documents/MIC3Spring2015Newsletter_FINAL_000.pdf*.

Military Interstate Children's Compact Commission. (2018). Interstate compact on educational opportunity for military children (Compact Rules Adopted November 2009, amended October 17, 2018). Retrieved from *www.mic3.net/assets/rules-2018-revised-9-nov-2018.pdf*.

Military Interstate Children's Compact Commission. (n.d.). *Interstate compact on educational opportunity for military children model compact language.* Lexington, KY: Author. Retrieved from *http://mic3.net/documents/InterstateCompactonEducationalOpportunityforMilitaryChildren-ModelLanguage.pdf*.

Military One Source. (2018a). What schools are available to children on military installations?

Retrieved from *www.militaryonesource.mil/education-employment/for-children-and-youth/pre-k-to-12-education/what-schools-are-available-to-children-on-military-installations*.

Military One Source. (2018b). The Exceptional Advocacy Newsletter Archives. Available at *www.militaryonesource.mil/the-exceptional-advocate-enewsletter-archives*

Military One Source. (2020a). Education Directory for Children with Special Needs. Retrieved from *https://efmpeducationdirectory.militaryonesource.mil*.

Military One Source. (2020b). The Exceptional Family Member Program: A program for families with special needs. Retrieved from *www.militaryonesource.mil/family-relationships/special-needs/exceptional-family-member/the-exceptional-family-member-program-for-families-with-special-needs*.

Military One Source. (n.d). Parenting and children resources. Retrieved from *www.militaryonesource.mil/family-relationships/parenting-and-children/parenting-and-children-resources*.

Military Parent Technical Assistance Center. (2017). Role of the school liaison officer. Retrieved from *https://branchta.org/role-school-liaison-officer-slo*.

Monson, C. M., & Fredman, S. J. (2012). *Cognitive-behavioral conjoint therapy for posttraumatic stress disorder: Harnessing the healing power of relationships.* New York: Guilford Press.

Morgan, M., & Ross, A. (2013). Helping military children feel at ease. Retrieved from *www.naesp.org/principal-janfeb-2013-teacher-staff-development/helping-military-children-feel-ease*.

Morin, A. (n.d.). Special education services for military families. Retrieved from *www.understood.org/en/school-learning/special-services/special-education-basics/special-education-services-for-military-families*.

Morris, A. S., & Age, T. R. (2009). Adjustment among youth in military families: The protective roles of effortful control and maternal social support. *Journal of Applied Developmental Psychology, 30*, 695–707.

Muller, R., Tong, F., & Irby, B. J. (2016). The military student identifier: A Texas study. *On the Move, 11*(1), 10–14. Retrieved from *www.militarychild.org/upload/files/resources/MSI_Insert.pdfhttps://www.militarychild.org/upload/files/resources/MSI_Insert.pdf*.

National Assessment of Educational Progress. (2018a). NAEP Reading Report Card. Retrieved from *www.nationsreportcard.gov/reading_2017?grade=4*.

National Assessment of Educational Progress. (2018b). NAEP Mathematics Report Card. Retrieved from *www.nationsreportcard.gov/math_2017?grade=4*.

National Association of School Psychologists. (2009a). *Appropriate Academic Supports to Meet the Needs of All Students* [Position Statement]. Bethesda, MD: Author.

National Association of School Psychologists. (2009b). *Appropriate Behavioral, Social, and Emotional Supports to Meet the Needs of All Students* [Position Statement]. Bethesda, MD: Author.

National Association of School Psychologists. (2015). *School psychologists: Qualified health professionals providing child and adolescent mental and behavioral health services* [White Paper]. Bethesda, MD: Author.

National Association of School Psychologists. (2016). NASP communities: Military families. Retrieved from *http://communities.nasponline.org/home*.

National Association of School Psychologists. (2020). *The Professional Standards of the National Association of School Psychologists.* Bethesda, MD: Author.

National Child Traumatic Stress Network. (2012). TF-CBT Trauma-focused cognitive behavioral therapy. Retrieved from *www.nctsn.org/sites/default/files/interventions/tfcbt_fact_sheet.pdf*.

National Child Traumatic Stress Network. (2018). TGCTA: Trauma and grief component therapy for adolescents. Retrieved from *www.nctsn.org/sites/default/files/interventions/tgcta_fact_sheet.pdf*.

National Defense Authorization Act for Fiscal Year 2016. (2015, November 25). Public Law 114-92.

National Governors Association Center for Best Practices & Council of Chief State School Officers. (2010). *Common Core Standards for English language arts and literacy in history/social studies, science, and technical subjects.*. Washington, DC: Author.

National Military Family Association. (2020). Military child education. Retrieved from *www.militaryfamily.org/info-resources/education*.

National Military Family Association. (n.d.). Operation Purple Camp. Retrieved from *https://www.militaryfamily.org/programs/operation-purple*.

National School Climate Center. (2015). Shared leadership across contexts. Retrieved from *www.schoolclimate.org/about/our-approach*.

Non-DoD Schools Program. (n.d.). Sponsor online orientation. Retrieved from *https://docplayer.net/6738234-Non-dod-schools-program.html*.

Ohye, B. Y., Jakubovic, R. S., Zakarian, R., & Bui, E. (2020). Staying strong with schools: Testing an elementary school-based intervention for military-connected children. *Journal of Clinical Child and Adolescent Psychology, 49*(5), 595–602.

Osofsky, J. D., & Molinda Chartrand, M. (2013). Military children from birth to five years. *The Future of Children, 23*(2), 61–77.

Palmer, C. (2008). A theory of risk and resilience factors in military families. *Military Psychology, 20*(3), 205–217.

Park, N. (2011). Military children and families: Strengths and challenges during peace and war. *American Psychologist, 66*(1), 65–72.

Pynoos, R. S. (1992). Grief and trauma in children and adolescents. *Bereavement Care, 11*, 2–10.

Pynoos, R. S., Layne, C. M., & Kaplow, J. B. (2012). Building developmentally-informed theory to support evidence-based assessment and treatment for bereaved youth. In C. M. Layne (Ed.), *Integrating developmentally-informed theory, evidence-based assessment, and evidence-based treatment of childhood maladaptive grief.* Symposium presented at the International Society for Traumatic Stress Studies meeting, Los Angeles, CA.

Pynoos, R. S., Steinberg, A. M., & Wraith, R. (1995). A developmental model of childhood traumatic stress. In D. Cicchetti & D. J. Cohen (Eds.), *Developmental psychopathology: Vol. 2. Risk, disorder, and adaptation* (pp. 72–95). New York: Wiley.

Reivich, K., & Shatte, A. (2002). *A resilience factor: Seven essential skills for overcoming life's inevitable obstacles.* New York: Broadway Books.

Richardson, A., Chandra, A., Martin, L. T., Setodji, C. M., Hallmark, B. W., Campbell, N. F., et al. (2011). *Effects of soldiers' deployment on children's academic performance and behavioral health.* Santa Monica, CA: RAND Corporation.

Rosenfield, S. A., & Humphrey, C. F. (2012). Consulting psychology in education: Challenge and change. *Consulting Psychology Journal: Practice and Research, 64*(1), 1–7.

Ruff, S. B., & Keim, M. A. (2014). Revolving doors: The impact of multiple school transitions on military children. *The Professional Counselor, 4*(2), 103–113.

Russo, T. J., & Fallon, M. A. (2015). Coping with stress: Supporting the needs of military families and their children. *Early Childhood Education Journal, 43*, 407–416.

Saltzman, W., Layne, C. M., Pynoos, R., Olafson, E., Kaplow, J., & Boat, B. (2017). *Trauma and grief component therapy for adolescents: A modular approach to treating traumatized and bereaved youth.* New York: Cambridge University Press.

Saltzman, W. R., Layne, C. M., Steinberg, A. M., & Pynoos, R. S. (2003). School-based trauma and grief-focused intervention for adolescents exposed to community violence. *Prevention Researcher, 10,* 8–11.

Sandomierski, T., Kincaid, D., & Algozzine, B. (2007). Response to intervention and positive behavior support: Brothers from different mothers or sisters with different misters? *Positive Behavioral Interventions and Supports Newsletter, 4*(2), 1–4.

Sammons, M. T., & Batten, S. V. (2008). Psychological services for returning veterans and their families: Evolving conceptualizations of the sequelae of war-zone experiences. *Journal of Clinical Psychology, 64,* 921–927.

School Superintendents Association. (2019). Fact sheet on the military child. Retrieved from *www.aasa.org/content.aspx?id=8998.*

Schuchs-Gopaul, E. L. (n.d.). Legal issues facing military families with special needs children: A primer and introduction. *The Reporter,* pp. 20–27. Retrieved from *www.wrightslaw.com/info/mil.parents.12things.pdf.*

Seal, K. H., Metzler, T. J., Gima, K. S., Berthenthal, D., Maguen, S., & Marmar, C. R. (2009). Trends and risk factors for mental health diagnoses among Iraq and Afghanistan Veterans using Department of Veterans Affairs health care, 2002–2008. *American Journal of Public Health, 99,* 1651–1658.

Section 504 of the Rehabilitation Act of 1973, 34 C.F.R. Part 104.

Sesame Workshop. (2019). Sesame Street for military families. Retrieved from *https://sesamestreetformilitaryfamilies.org.*

Sheppard, S. C., Malatras, J. W., & Israel, A. C. (2010). The impact of deployment on U.S. military families. *American Psychologist, 65*(6), 599–609.

Sherman, M. D., & Glenn, M. A. (2011). Opportunities for school psychologists working with children of military families. *Communiqué, 39*(5), 1, 17–19.

Shinn, M. R. (2010). Building a scientifically based data system for progress monitoring and universal screening across three tiers including RTI using curriculum-based measurement. In M. R. Shinn & H. M. Walker (Eds.), *Interventions for achievement and behavior problems in a three-tier model, including RTI* (pp. 259–292). Bethesda, MD: National Association of School Psychologists.

Shinn, M. R. (2013). Identifying and validating academic problems. In R. Brown-Chidsey & K. J. Andren (Ed.). *Assessment for intervention: A problem-solving approach* (2nd ed., pp. 199–228). New York: Guilford Press.

Siegel, B. S., Davis, B. E., & the Committee on Psychosocial Aspects of Child and Family Functioning and Section on Uniformed Services. (2013). Health and mental health needs of children in military families. *Pediatrics, 131*(6), 2002–2015.

Skalski, A. K., Minke, K., Rossen, E., Cowan, K. C., Kelly, J., Armistead, R., et al. (2015). *NASP Practice Model Implementation Guide.* Bethesda, MD: National Association of School Psychologists.

Smrekar, C., Guthrie, J. W., Owens, D. E., & Sims, P. G. (2001). *March toward excellence: School success and minority student achievement in Department of Defense schools: A report to the National Education Goals Panel.* Washington, DC: National Education Goals Panel.

Smrekar, C. E., & Owens, D. E. (2003). "It's a way of life for us": High mobility and high achievement in Department of Defense Schools. *Journal of Negro Education, 72*(1), 165–177.

Sogomonyan, F., & Cooper, J. L. (2010). Trauma faced by children of military families: What every policymaker should know. Retrieved from *www.nccp.org/wp-content/uploads/2010/05/text_938.pdf*.

Splitek, D. F. (2016). The military student identifier. *On the Move, 10*(2), 40. Retrieved from *OTM 10-2016-final-highres.pdf*.

State of Florida. (2011). Guiding tools for instructional problem solving (GTIPS). Retrieved from *www.florida-rti.org/_docs/GTIPS.pdf*.

State of Florida's MTSS. (2012). MTSS implementation components. Ensuring common language and understanding. Retrieved from *www.florida-rti.org/educatorResources/MTSS_Book_ImplComp_012612.pdf*.

State of Washington, Office of Superintendent of Public Instruction. (2015). *Graduation alternatives*. Olympia, WA: Author. Retrieved from *www.k12.wa.us/assessment/GraduationAlternatives/#waiver*.

State of Washington, Office of Superintendent of Public Instruction. (n.d.). *Washington State Graduation Requirements*. Olympia, WA: Author. Retrieved from *www.k12.wa.us/GraduationRequirements/default.aspx*.

Stepka, P., & Callahan, K. (2016). The impact of military life on young children and their parents. In A. H. Gewirtz & A. M. Youssef (Eds.), *Risk and resilience in military and veteran families: Parenting and children's resilience in military families* (pp. 11–26). Cham, Switzerland: Springer International.

Stiller, B. C., Nese, R. N. T., Tomlanovich, A. K., Horner, R. H., & Ross, S. W. (2013). *Bullying and harassment prevention in positive behavior support: Expect respect*. Eugene: University of Oregon.

Stoiber, K. C. (2014). A comprehensive framework for multitiered systems of support in school psychology. In P. L. Harrison & A. Thomas (Eds.), *Best practices in school psychology* (pp. 41–70). Bethesda, MD: National Association of School Psychologists.

Sumner, J., Boisvert, D., & Andersen, J. P. (2016). The effects of stress and social support on externalizing behaviors among children in military families. *Deviant Behavior, 37*(3), 246–262.

Tandon, M., Cardeli, E., & Luby, J. (2009). Internalizing disorders in early childhood: A review of depressive and anxiety disorders. *Child and Adolescent Psychiatric Clinics of North America, 18*(3), 593–610.

Towhey, J. R. (2018, April 26). Students at Defense Department schools outperform peers in public schools. Retrieved from *www.insidesources.com/students-defense-department-schools-outperform-peers-public-schools*.

Trauma-Focused Cognitive Behavioral Therapy National Therapist Certification Program. (2020). TF-CBT military implementation resources. Retrieved from *https://tfcbt.org/tf-cbt-military-implementation-resources*.

Trautmann, J., Alhusen, J., & Gross, D. (2015). Impact of deployment on military families with young children: A systematic review. *Nursing Outlook, 6*(3), 656–679.

University of Missouri Evidence-Based Intervention Network. (2015). Behavioral assessment screening: I need to identify who is in need of extra help. Retrieved from *http://ebi.missouri.edu/?cat=46*.

U.S. Department of Defense, (2009). National Defense Authorization Act for fiscal year 2010, Section 563 Public Law 111-84. Retrieved from *www.govinfo.gov/content/pkg/PLAW-111publ84/pdf/PLAW-111publ84.pdf* https://download.militaryonesource.mil/12038/Project%20Documents/MCFP/eMagazine/NDAA_563.pdf.

U.S. Department of Defense. (2014). Department of Defense Directory: Early Intervention, Special Education and Related Services in OCONUS Communities—DoD Dependents Schools and Educational Developmental Intervention Services. Retrieved from *https://download.militaryonesource.mil/12038/Project%20Documents/MilitaryHOMEFRONT/Troops%20and%20Families/Special%20Needs%20EFMP/OCONUS_Directory.pdf*.

U.S. Department of Defense. (2015). Provision of early intervention and special education services to eligible DoD dependents: Final rule. *Federal Register, 80*(122), 32 Code of Federal Regulations (CFR), Part 57, pp. 36654–36688.

U.S. Department of Defense. (2016). Demographics profile of the military community. Retrieved from *download.militaryonesource.mil/12038/MOS/Reports/2016-Demographics-Report.pdf*.

U.S. Department of Defense Education Activity. (2019a). The Month of the Military Child. Retrieved from *www.dodea.edu/dodeaCelebrates/Military-Child-Month.cfm*.

U.S. Department of Defense Education Activity. (2019b). School liaison officers. Retrieved from *www.dodea.edu/Partnership/schoolLiaisonOfficers.cfm*.

U.S. Department of Defense Education Activity. (2019c). School accreditation reports. Retrieved from *www.dodea.edu/Accreditation/standards.cfm*.

U.S. Department of Defense Education Activity. (2019d). DoDEA accreditation frequently asked questions. Retrieved from *www.dodea.edu/Accreditation/FAQ.cfm*.

U.S. Department of Defense Education Activity. (2019e). DoDEA Accreditation Reports System (DARS). Retrieved from *https://webapps.dodea.edu/DARS/Home.cfm*.

U.S. Department of Defense Education Activity. (2019f). DoDEA College and Career Ready Standards. Retrieved from *www.ed.gov/k-12reforms/standards*.

U.S. Department of Defense Education Activity. (2019g). Curricular programs. Retrieved from *www.dodea.edu/Curriculum/index.cfm*.

U.S. Department of Defense Education Activity. (2019h). DoDEA graduation requirements. Retrieved from *www.dodea.edu/collegeCareerReady/graduation-requirements.cfm.*.

U.S. Department of Defense Education Activity. (2019i). Non-DoD Schools Program Orientation. Retrieved from *https://content.dodea.edu/teach_learn/partnership/ndsp/ndsp_orientation/index.html*.

U.S. Department of Defense Education Activity. (2019j). Locating schools. Retrieved from *www.dodea.edu/nonDoD/resources/locatingschools.cfm*.

U.S. Department of Defense Education Activity. (2019k). Choosing an international school. Retrieved from *www.dodea.edu/nonDoD/upload/choosinginternationalschools.pdf*.

U.S. Department of Defense Education Activity. (2019l). Non-English school guidance. Retrieved from *www.dodea.edu/nonDoD/upload/NonEnglishSchoolGuidance.pdf*.

U.S. Department of Defense Education Activity. (2019m). Home study education plan. Retrieved from *www.dodea.edu/nonDoD/upload/Home-Study-Private-Instruction-Education-Plan.pdf*.

U.S. Department of Defense Exceptional Family Member Program. (2014). Special needs parent tool kit: Birth to 18. Retrieved from *https://download.militaryonesource.mil/12038/EFMP/PTK_SCORs/ParentToolkit_Apr2014.pdf*.

U.S. Department of Education. (2008). Policy questions on the Department of Education's 2007 guidance on collecting, maintaining and reporting data by race or ethnicity. Retrieved from *www2.ed.gov/policy/rschstat/guid/raceethnicity/questions.html*.

U.S. Department of Education. (2009). Accrediting agencies recognized by the U.S. Department of Education. Retrieved from *www2.ed.gov/students/prep/college/diplomamills/accreditation.html*.

U.S. Department of Education. (n.d.). College and Career Ready Standards. Retrieved from *www.ed.gov/k-12reforms/standards*.

U.S. Department of Education, International Affairs Office. (2007). *Accreditation and quality assurance: School level accreditation*. Washington, DC: Author.

U.S. Department of Education, Office of Special Education and Rehabilitative Services (2013). Dear State Director of Special Education. Retrieved from *www2.ed.gov/policy/speced/guid/idea/memosdcltrs/12-0392dclhighlymobile.pdf*.

Vaillancourt Strobach, K. (2015). *The Every Student Succeeds Act and school psychologists*. Bethesda, MD: National Association of School Psychologists. Retrieved from *www.nasponline.org/research-and-policy/policy-matters/the-every-student-succeeds-act-and-school-psychologists*.

VanDerHeyden, A. (n.d.). Approaches to RTI: Selecting an RTI model. Retrieved from *www.rtinetwork.org/learn/what/approaches-to-rti*.

Varni, J. W., Burwinkle, T. M., & Seid, M. (2006). The Peds QL™ 4.0 as a school population health measure: Feasibility, reliability and validity. *Quality of Life Research, 15*(2), 203–215.

Walker, H. M., & Severson, H. (1992). *Systematic screening for behavior disorders* (2nd ed.). Longmont, CO: Sopris West.

Walker, H. Severson, H. H., Feil, E. (2014). *Systematic screening for behavior disorders (SSBD) technical manual universal screening for pre-K–9*. Eugene, OR: Pacific Northwest.

Weber, E. G., & Weber, D. K. (2005). Geographic relocation frequency, resilience, and military adolescent behavior. *Military Medicine, 170*(7), 638–642.

Werber, L., Schaefer, A. G., Osilla, K. C., Wilke, E., Wong, A., Breslau, J., et al. (2013). *Support for the 21st century reserve force: Insights on facilitating successful reintegration for citizen warriors and their families*. Santa Monica, CA: RAND Corporation.

Workforce Democrats Reauthorization of the Elementary and Secondary Education Act Conference Report on S.1177, the Every Student Succeeds Act. (2015). Retrieved from *http://larsen.house.gov/sites/larsen.house.gov/files/documents/Every%20Student%20Succeeds%20Act%20detailed%20fact%20sheet.pdf*.

Wright, P. W. D., & Wright, P. D. (2008). Child Find. Retrieved from *www.wrightslaw.com/info/child.find.index.htm*.

Wright, P. W. D., & Wright, P. D. (2015). Military and Department of Defense (DoD) special education. Retrieved from *www.wrightslaw.com/info/dod.index.htm*.

Youth in Mind. (2007). SDQ: *Information for researchers and professionals about the Strengths and Difficulties Questionnaire*. Retrieved from *www.sdqinfo.com*.

Index

Academic screening, with MTSS, 28
Accreditation, for DoD schools, 17–18
Accrediting agencies, US, 17
Adolescence, social development during, 55–57
Advocacy
   resources for, 105, 111t
   school psychologist's role in, 116
After Deployment Adaptive Parenting Tools (ADAPT), 9–10, 38, 39t, 77–78, 79
Americans with Disabilities Act (ADA), 99
Autism spectrum disorder (ASD), school transitions and, 86, 87, 89–90

B

Behavioral and Emotional Screening System (BASC-3 BESS), 29
Behavioral concerns, in deployment situations, 75
Behavioral screening, with MTSS, 28–29
Black students, in DoDEA schools, 19–20
Boys and Girls Clubs of America, 56t
Building Capacity and Welcoming Practices in Military-Connected Schools, 2
Bullying, case example of MTSS approach to, 40–42

Bullying and Harassment Prevention in Positive Behavior Support: Expect Respect handbook, 40–41

C

California Healthy Kids Survey, 6–7, 65
   data from, 34
   military-specific modules and, 32
Caregivers, of infants and preschool children, 49
Child and Adolescent Social Support Scale, 53
Child attachment, 49
Child Find, 7, 50, 118
Child maltreatment, parental deployment and, 75–76
Civilian middle school, case example of MTSS approach, 40–42
Civilian schools, 11–17
   awareness of military students in, 13–14
   fictional family snapshot and, 16–17
   guiding questions for, 15t
   local context/cultural considers and, 16
   mental health support in, 64
   support of military students in, 14, 16
Civilian settings, public schools in, 12–17

Cognitive-behavioral interventions, 68–71
  for internalizing disorders, stress, trauma, 68
  for traumatic grief, 68–71
Cognitive-behavioral therapy (CBT)
  for mental health interventions, 72t–73t
  trauma-focused, 69, 72t–73t, 79
Collaborative for Academic, Social, and Emotional Learning (CASEL), 65–66
Community culture, and military students in public schools, 16
Comprehensive Integrated Three-Tiered Model of Prevention (Ci3T), 29
Curriculum-based measures (CBMs), 6
  MTSS and, 28

D

Data-based decision making, school psychologists and, 7–10
Decision rules, application of, 29–30
Department of Defense Education Activity (DoDEA)
  non-DoD schools and, 12
  school statistics of, 12
  website of, 17
Department of State Standardized Regulations (DSSR), 24
Deployment; *see* Military deployment
Developmental systems theory (DST), 4–5
Difficulties Questionnaire, 29
Disabilities; *see also* Special education
  military youth with, school transitions and, 85–87, 88t, 89–90
DoD Directory, special education/disability resources in, 88t, 89
DoD summer camps, 59t
DoDEA Program orientation document, 22, 23t, 24
DoDEA schools, 17–22
  academic achievement in, 19–20
  accreditation, curriculum, graduation requirements, 18t
  accreditation of, 17–18, 18t
  advantages of, 83
  characteristics of, 20–21
  fictional family snapshot of, 21–22
  graduation requirements of, 18–19
  locations of, 12
  mental health support and, 64
  teachers in, 20
  world distribution of, 17

E

Early childhood
  data collection and, 7–10
  military deployment and, 51
  social development during, 48–51
Educational and Developmental Intervention Services (EDIS), 83, 86, 93–94
Educational settings, 11–26; *see also* Civilian schools; DoDEA schools; Non-DoD schools
Elementary and Secondary Education Act, 100
Elementary school students, social development of, 51–54
Emotional concerns, in deployment situations, 75
Emotional screening, with MTSS, 28–29
Erikson, Erik, 47
Erikson's social development theory, 48–57
  stage 1: infancy, 48
  stage 2: autonomy, 48
  stage 3: initiative *versus* guilt, 48–51, 50t
  stage 4: industry *versus* inferiority, 51–54
  stage 5: identity *versus* isolation, 55
  stage 6: young adulthood, 55
  stage 7: generativity *versus* stagnation, 55–57
  stage 8: integrity *versus* despair, 55–57
Every Student Succeeds Act (ESSA), 99, 100–104, 118
  accountability and data requirements, 100
  and awareness of military students, 13
  disaggregated subgroup military data and, 100–101
  DoD-specific special education regulations, 103–104
  and identifying military students, 13–14
  impact aid, 102–103
  reporting requirements of, 30–31
  special education legislation and provisions, 103
  specialized instructional support personnel defined, 101–102
Evidence-Based Intervention (EBI) group, 29
Exceptional Advocate, The, description and link, 111t
Exceptional Advocate Newsletter Archives, 105

Exceptional Family Member Program (EFMP), 86, 87, 95
 description and link, 111t
 guide to, 104
 purpose of, 104–105
Extracurricular activities
 military youth and, 56–57
 school transitions and, 90–91

F

Families
 military deployments and, 2 (*see also* Military deployments)
 military history of, 32
 military transition impacts and, 47
Families OverComing Under Stress (FOCUS), 9–10, 38, 39t, 77–78
Family stressors, deployment and, 76–77
Federal Special Education Regulations, description and link, 111t

G

Good Grief Program for Bereaved Military Children, 69
Grief, traumatic, CBT and, 68–71
Grief counseling, 116
 case example, 78–81

I

Impact Aid, ESSA and, 102–103
Individuals with Disabilities Education Act (IDEA), 99
 special education categories of, 104
Infants, social development of, 48–51
Internalizing disorders, CBT interventions for, 68
Interstate Compact on Educational Opportunity for Military Children (ICEOMC), 85

L

Latinx students, in DoDEA schools, 19–20
Legal aspects; *see* Legislation

Legal resources; *see also* Legislation; specific legislation
 information on, 111t
Legislation, 99–111; *see also* specific legislation
 Every Student Succeeds Act, 100–104
 examples of, 99
 Military Interstate Children's Compact, 105–110, 107t
 National Defense Authorization Act, 104–105
 relevance of, 118–119

M

Mental health interventions, service branch factors and, 74
Mental health professionals, school-based, 50–51
Mental health supports, 61–81
 case example, 78–81
 military deployments and, 71, 74–78
  child maltreatment risk, 75–76
  deployment characteristics, 74–75
  emotional/behavioral assessments, 75
  family stressors, 76–77
  support during, 77–78
 Tier 1/universal applications, 61–67
  classroom-based, 65–67
  school climate, 64–65
  social relationships/connections, 61–64
 Tiers 2 and 3/specialized needs, 67–71, 72t–73t
  cognitive-behavioral, 68–71
  wraparound support, 71
Military Child Education Coalition (MCEC), 13, 53, 93, 100
 Reserve and National Guard members and, 31
Military Child Education Coalition Ted Talks, 59t
Military culture, training in, 35–36, 37t
Military deployment
 cycle of, educating school personnel about, 116
 factors related to mental health issues, 74–75
 with families, 2
 family and youth support and, 77–78
 unique early childhood experiences and, 51
Military families, strengths and assets of, 3
Military Interstate Children's Compact, 16–17, 82, 84–85, 105–110, 107t
 case examples of applications, 108
 critical role of, 118–119
 description and link, 111t

Military Interstate Children's Compact *(cont.)*
    provisions and district responsibilities, 107t
    provisions 6f, 105
    students and others covered by, 105
Military Interstate Children's Compact Commission, 99, 106
Military Kids Connect, 56t
Military One Source, 50t, 88t, 104–105
Military One Source website, 87
Military Student Transition Consultants (MSTC), 94
Military transitions; *see also* School transitions
impacts on social development and relationships, 46–47
Military youth
    data collection specific to, 32
    defining, 31–32
    demographics of, 83
    educational settings of, 83
    guidance for schools, 2
    identifying, 13–14
    individual support for, 39
    multi-tiered systems of support for, 5–10
    ongoing recognition of, 54
    prevalence of, 1–2
    school psychologist role *(see* School psychologist)
    strengths and assets of, 3
    strengths-based resiliency approach and, 3–5
    support in public schools, 14, 15t, 16
    supportive activities and initiatives for, 56t–57t
    website resources for, 97
Military youth with disabilities
    resources for, 86, 88t
    school transitions and, 85–87, 89–90
Minority students, in DoDEA schools, 19–20
Multidimensional Grief Theory, 69–71
Multi-Tiered Systems of Support (MTSS), 5–10, 27–45
    and adaptations for military youth, 113–114
    adolescents and, 57
    and application of decision rules, 29–30
    applications to military youth and families, 6–7
    case example in civilian middle school, 40–42
    decision rules and, 29–30
    ESSA and, 102 *(see also* Every Student Succeeds Act [ESSA])
    family service/educational history form, 43–46
    general principles of, 27–28
    school psychologists and, 7–10
    secondary/tier 2 systems of support, 38, 39t
    tertiary/tier 3 special considerations, 39
    universal screening and, 28–29
    universal/tier 1 screening and support, 30–37, 116
        online training/development, 37t
        practice considerations, 34
        problem-solving considerations, 34–36
        procedural considerations, 33

N

National Assessment of Educational Progress (NAEP), school performance ratings of, 19, 83
National Association of School Psychologists (NASP), 92
National Council on Disability (NCD), 85–86
National Defense Authorization Act, 104–105
    ESSA and, 103
National Guard
    deployments of, 74
    social supports and, 47
    youth mental health and, 64
National Military Family Association, 100, 101
Non-DoD schools, 22–25
    DoDEA and, 12
    fictional family snapshot of, 24–25
    funding in overseas locations, 22–23
    list of, 23t
    mental health support and, 64
    web resources of, 23t
Non-DoD Schools Program (NDSP), 22

O

Obama, Barack, 100
Office discipline referrals (ODRs), 28, 35, 41
Operation Purple Buddy Camp, 56t, 75

P

Parent liaisons, 41
Parenting Stress Index (PSI), 76
Parents, support for, 39t, 49, 50t
Pediatric Symptom Checklist, 76
Penn Resilience Program, 72t

Posttraumatic stress disorder (PTSD), parental, 51
Preschool experiences, facilitating, 49–51, 50t
Provision of Early Intervention (DoD), 99
Psychologists; *see* School psychologist
PTSD, parental, 51
Public schools; *see* Civilian schools; non-DoD schools
Purple Up Campaign, 54
    DoDEA and, 12
Purple Up for Military Kids, 54
Purple Up Month of the Military Child, 59t

R

Rehabilitation Act of 1973, 99
Relationships, and impacts of military transitions, 46–47
Reserves
    deployments of, 74
    social supports and, 47
    youth mental health and, 64
Resiliency approach, 4–5; *see also* Strengths-based/resiliency model
    school transitions and, 92

S

School climate
    measures of, 36
    mental health support and, 64–65
School connectedness, case example of MTSS approach and, 40–42
School psychologist
    consultation and collaboration by, 94–97
    EFMP and, 95
    ESSA and, 101–102
    and ESSA data collection, 114–115
    and familiarity with DoDEA and Civilian school systems, 93
    and knowledge of school settings, 113–114
    mental health support issues and, 63–64
    and military deployment considerations, 71, 74–78
    MTSS data-based decision making and, 7–10
    research contributions of, 114, 118
    resources for, 88t, 92–93
    role in public schools, 12–13
    role in strengths-based MTSS model, 112–113
    role in youth social development, 115
    support by, 41–42
    and support during transitions, 91–94
    support role of, 2–3
School settings; *see* Civilian schools; DoDEA schools; Non-DoD schools
School transitions, 82–98
    considerations for youth with disabilities, 85–87, 88t, 89–90
    consultation and collaboration lens and, 94–97
    extracurricular activities and, 90–91
    families' experiences of, 84
    frequency of, 83–84
    impacts of, 46–47
    Military Interstate Children's Compact and, 84–85
    school psychologist's role in, 91–94, 117
School-age military youth; *see* Military youth
Schools
    DoDEA and non-DoD, 12
    guidance for, 2
    public (*see* Civilian schools; Non-DoD schools)
Schoolwide Evaluation Tool (SET), 64
Schoolwide Positive Behavior Support (SWPBS), 64, 65
    ESSA and, 102
Screening instruments, 29
SELect program, 66
Sesame Street for Military Families, 50t
Social, Academic, and Emotional Behavior Risk Screener, 29
Social development, 46–60
    of elementary school students, 51–54
    school psychologist's role in, 115
    social developmental theory and, 48–59
    social supports and, 47
    supports across developmental spectrum, 60
Social developmental theory, 48–59
Social relationships, mental health support and, 61–64
Social worker, support by, 41
Social-emotional screening, MTSS team and, 116
Special education
    DoD Directory resources and, 88t
    information and resources on, 111t
    support for, 117–118
Special education legislation, ESSA and, 103
Special education regulations, DoD-specific, 103–104

Special Education Services to Eligible DoD Dependents (DoD), 99
Special Needs Parent Toolkit, 88t
Specialized instructional support personnel (SISP), 102
Stay Strong with Schools, 53
Strengths-based/resiliency model, 3–4
    case study, 8–10
    MTSS adaptations for military youth and, 113
    MTSS and, 112
    versus "pathologizing" military youth, 116
    school psychologists' leadership and, 112–113
Stress, CBT interventions for, 68
Student Risk Screening Scale for Early Childhood, 29
Student Risk Screening Scale—Internalizing and Externalizing, 29
Student 2 Student, 59t
Sure Start Preschool, 49–50
Systematic Screening for Behavior Disorders, 29

T

Teachers, in DoD schools, 20
Ted Talks, Military Child Education Coalition and, 59t

Tragedy Assistance Program for Survivors (TAPS) Good Grief Camps, 69, 73t
Trauma, CBT interventions for, 68
Trauma and grief component therapy for adolescents (TGCTA), 70–71, 73t
Trauma-focused cognitive-behavioral therapy (TF-CBT), 69, 72t–73t, 79
Traumatic grief, CBT and, 68–71

U

US Department of Education (DoE), DoD schools and, 17

V

Virtual high schools, 17

W

White students, in DoDEA schools, 20
Wraparound planning, 71, 80
Wrightslaw, description and link, 111t
Wrightslaw website, 104